A Traveller's Life

Sheila Stewart MBE

Foreword by
Jess Smith

BIRLINN

First published in 2011 by
Birlinn Limited
West Newington House
10 Newington Road
Edinburgh
EH9 1QS

www.birlinn.co.uk

Copyright © Sheila Stewart, 2011
Foreword © Jess Smith, 2011

ISBN-13: 978 1 84158 979 4

British Library Cataloguing-in-Publication Data
A catalogue record for this book is available from the British
Library

Set in Bembo at Birlinn

Printed and bound in Great Britain by
Cox & Wyman, Reading

Contents

Illustrations

Me at the age of 4

My Uncle Donald, who taught me the ballads

Travellers in their camp

My father, Alex Stewart, with his bagpipes

Me at the age of 10

My Uncle Hendry playing the pipes

Winning the Miss Christmas competition

My mother and me

Hamish Henderson, the first time he came to see us

Ian and me on our wedding day

Me in Hatfield in the 1960s

Me with Roy

The Stewarts o' Blair at Lake Como, Italy

My mother with me on her 90th birthday

Foreword
by Jess Smith

❧

Although we had seldom met, Sheila Stewart of the Stewarts of Blair had always been a part of my life, from the time of our yearly visits to the berries where her voice, and that of Cathie, her sister, and mother, Belle, could be heard across the berryfields. They rang out from among the high bushy canes of the Norfolk drills, where the fruit was the size of your fist and it took up to a week to gather it in.

I remember them singing bawdy songs, funny and sad songs and long ballads. They would set riddles and, most of all, provide guid crack. A joyous concert all for free! A human radio while we worked, broadcasting endless fun which was continued at the day's end on the green around blazing camp-fires.

Sheila was the voice of Blairgowrie and the vibrant heart of Scotland's travelling folk, a raven–haired beauty, envy of many traveller lassies, and the dream girl of the laddies. More importantly, she was her uncle Donald's protégée; she was aged only five when he recognised in this child the one who would be the carrier of the ballad tradition of the travelling people.

For me, a mere tinker berry-picker, the most vivid memory to come out of Blair was that of Sheila and her perfect voice. This was the time when Maurice Fleming, a journalist from the area, contacted folklorist Hamish Henderson and excitedly informed him, 'I have found the voices of two angels.' He was referring to Belle and Sheila.

Hamish introduced himself to them, and from that association emerged Scotland's until then hidden treasure; the Stewarts of Blair. Father Alex with his bagpipes and sister Cathy rounded off a complete family act.

Time passed, and as each member of the famous group died, Sheila, like the Dewars, keepers of the relics of saints in olden days, stood alone and carried the banner of her traditional culture high. It was a massive responsibility, a position which would have proved impossible for her to sustain if it were not for the joy of children coming to add their help and the happy home she created.

Although Sheila had always been part of my culture, it was in Cromarty about ten years ago, at a traditional singing and story weekend, that we first met as individuals. She had lost her train tickets, and since Dave, my husband, and I were heading to Perthshire, a short detour behind Dunkeld, over by Butterstone and on to Blairgowrie, wouldn't take us that far out of our way.

Our mode of transport, however, left a lot to be desired. Dave's very small and basic work van had only two seats. With Sheila being that little bit older than me for a start, and what's more, she being our guest, into the back I went. Settling down among work tools, including seriously sharp chainsaws, hammers and God alone knew what else my man had heaped in there, I was under no illusion that my journey down the length of the A9 was going to be a comfortable one. But as it turned out, I was wrong.

It had been a long time since I'd had a conversation with one of my own kind – a colourful, Perthshire traveller, and a famous one at that! As I sat hunched up in the back, gazing through the dog grille separating us, Sheila and I, like rivers in spate, poured forth our stories, riddles and songs. We laughed at our memories of certain tinker worthies; in fact we cried with laughter. Not once did we mention time, weather or the price of fuel.

Before I had time to consider my painful backside or any other part of my anatomy, we solemnly promised to keep in touch. From that heartwarming oath came a friendship which has stood the test of time; we have never let a single day pass without phoning and sharing our lives, and have become true sisters in the blood.

We have shared stages and school classrooms, where we bring our culture to life with those of future generations in the hope that when they are adults they might change attitudes and lift the veil of propaganda which has covered our culture for hundreds of years. Sheila has worked tirelessly to achieve this, and indeed many traveller sites through out Britain now have her stamp on them. Consulting over the years with councils and government officials, Sheila has spent months away from home, speaking out for the downtrodden travelling folk who remain close to her heart.

'I was born a traveller,' she reminds her audiences, then continues, 'and I shall be one till the day I die.' And when illness sneaked in and tried to cut the cord between her and Mother Earth, it was that finale she thought she was facing. But with the heart of a lioness, she bravely fought her ill health and overpowered it.

Through everything, it is her love of the ballads which has remained her top priority. Her workshops are fantastic events, where participants leave rejuvenated, bursting with the 'heart music', or, as Sheila so poignantly calls it, 'the conyach'.

When for the first time the late Pope John Paul II visited Scotland, Sheila was invited to sing at Bellahouston Park where he was addressing the faithful. Her singing so impressed the Holy Father he made a point of speaking to her. At the celebrations at the inauguration of President Ford in Washington DC she found once more an audience hypnotised by her songs. Prince Philip was so taken by her voice when she attended the US Bicentennial that he requested she give an impromptu performance to their royal highnesses.

I could go on, but Sheila wants to tell you all about these things herself. As you read through her autobiography, see what happens the time she meets the Indian chief!

In the past, when I was a traveller of the road, certain family members had hammered it into me that I shouldn't sing because I had no air to my voice. Sheila found that buried voice and gave it life; now I love to sing.

As an author writing about our culture, I in turn encouraged her to write the story of her own struggle to overcome prejudice and to tell her story to the world. Here then is that story, and I hope while reading it you gain a closer understanding of this songstress from the famous 'Stewarts o' Blair', the last in the line, and that she leaves a lasting impression on your heart.

Jess Smith

Preface

I have thought long and hard about a question I have often been asked. If you weren't a traveller, what would you like to be? My answer is, I wouldn't like to be anything else. Every morning I wake up, and every night I go to sleep, I thank God for making me what I am. If I had to live my life over, I wouldn't change a thing. The pleasure life as a traveller has given me is indescribable. To learn the culture of the travellers has been so fulfilling, I just can't put it into words. The travelling life is now slowly dying, but I am happy to have been part of the old ways.

Sheila Stewart

1
My Story Begins

I am going to start the story of my life two days before I was born. My parents were living with my mother's mother, my granny, and one day they had a big argument with her and she threw them out onto the street with nowhere to go.

My father was a good friend of the owner of the Angus Hotel in Blairgowrie, and asked him if he knew of anywhere where he and my mother could shelter till the baby was born.

'Well,' said the hotel-keeper, 'there is only one place I have to offer, but it may not suit you and your wife in her condition.'

'Anything will do us,' said my father. 'We have two children with us, a boy and a girl. Our oldest boy is staying with my wife's mother. We would be more than grateful for any place for ourselves.'

The owner looked at him long and hard and then said to him, 'Alright, Sandy, you can stay here. But the place is the stable at the back of the hotel. I sold the horses two weeks ago. You are welcome to go in there.'

My father was very grateful, and my parents moved into the stable two days before I was born.

When my mother's labour pains started, the man of the hotel found out about it and called Nurse Kidd, who was the midwife for Blairgowrie at that time. She came with much excitement, because she had never delivered a traveller's baby before.

I was born on 7 July 1935. I weighed in at two and a half pounds. The nurse thought I must be a twin and waited to see if another baby was to be born, but no, it was only me, there was no twin.

The nurse went away after seeing we were alright, and came back an hour later with clothes taken off a doll she had as a child. They were still too big for me, and she had to sew the hat in because it was too big for my head.

My mother called me Sheila after my granny's wee dog, a Pomeranian. So I was named after a dog, just because my mother liked the name.

A few days after I was born, granny came down to the stable and asked them to go back and stay with her, which they did. A couple of days after we got there, my mother wrapped me in a shawl, and she and my father walked to Blacklaw to pick raspberries, because they had no money. They picked all day to get food for themselves and my brother and sister. They did this for the whole berry season and saved some money.

The first thing I can remember is when I was about two. It was when I was staying with my uncle Donald, which I did on and off from when I was born. My first memory is of when my mother's cousin Andy took me by the hand down the road to Rattray Cross. Why we were there, I did not know, but I soon found out. Five minutes later a hearse came along with a coffin in it. Andy told me it was my granny (my mother's mother) who had died. She was being taken to Alyth to be buried, and I would never see her again.

At that age I didn't know what he was talking about, so for me life just went on as usual. It wasn't until I was older that I understood, and treasured that memory of being there to watch my granny's coffin pass. Then all the memories of the times I spent with my granny came back to me. I have held onto them all my life.

We spent many summers in tents going pearl-fishing and doing the harvest. It was our way of life and I didn't know anything else. To me there was no other world but the one I was living in.

I was about three when my mother taught me my first song. It was called 'Twa Heeds Are Better than Yin'. Here is the song:

Twa Heeds Are Better than Yin

Richt weel dae I mind on the days of lang syne,
When I was a laddie sae wee,
Whenever I'd gang, aye, and dae something wrong,
My mother would lecture tae me.

She would cry oot, 'My bairn, keep awa' fae a' herm,
Or ye'll rue it if aince you begin.
And never think twice for tae take an advice,
For twa heeds are aye better than yin.

Now when a young chiel aye intends tae dae weel,
Of course he looks oot for a wife,
A bonny wee tert wi' a true loving hert,
To sew on his buttons for life.

He calls her his plum, aye, his yummy, yum, yum,
And he tickles her under the chin,
And he whispers, 'My dear, let's get married next year,
For twa heeds are aye better than yin.'

When I had learned it she took me up to my uncle Donald's to show me off. When I sang the song to him he kissed me and gave me a half-crown, which was a lot of money then. My uncle Donald always seemed to have plenty of money. Where he got it, I didn't know then.

My mother was so pleased to get the half-crown, because she could buy groceries with it that lasted two days. There was method to my mother's madness. At three I was the family's breadwinner. She said this to my father and they had a good laugh about it.

I was small and slim at that age, and looked just like the golly on the tins of marmalade, and that is what my mother's uncle Hendry called me – 'The Marmalade Can'.

I may say I was spoiled by my family, especially by my brothers and my sister. I adored my brother John. He spoiled me the most. My brother Andy and me were always arguing about something, but in spite of this we had that special bond, different from anything else in the family. My sister Cathie was the housekeeper for us at that time, or should I say tent-keeper. She cleaned, washed the clothes and cooked while my mother was away hawking or working on farms with my father.

I can always remember I used to play a game with myself when I went to the shops with my mother or Cathie. Every house I passed, I used to imagine myself in it, especially if it was a big one, and wonder about the people who lived there. What were they like, not being travellers? What did they speak like, and what did they talk about?

One day my mother said to me, 'Sheila, the shows [fairground] are on in the mart yard. We are going to see Mrs Taylor about something, get your coat on.' Not suspecting anything, I did as she said. When we got up to Mrs Taylor's caravan she was sitting at the fire in front of it. She shouted to her son Danny as soon as I arrived. When he came to the fire she gave him a look and a nod, and he grabbed me and held me down. My mother had disappeared just then, and I didn't know where she was. I was screaming like a banshee, I will never forget that. They held me down and pierced my two ears with a darning needle and a potato. They put white thread through my ears to keep the holes open, and told me to put my spit on them every morning till they healed.

I never spoke to my mother for days after that. At the time we were living in my granny's house in Old Rattray after she had died. The next day a knock came to the door. It was Danny Taylor, come to see if I was alright. Well, I fled when he came in the door. I hid in my granny's shed round the side of the house, and my ankles were pecked to death by my granny's kya laddie. This is what we called the jackdaw she had instead of a dog to keep folk from her door. I was thinking to myself I would rather face the bird than face Danny Taylor again, God knows where he would pierce me next.

I huddled in a corner of the shed, until my mother appeared

and told me to come out. We never said no to my mother, it was just not done. I came out and went into the house. Danny said he had a present for me. My ears certainly pricked up when I heard the word present. He swept me up into his arms, kissed me on the cheek and said, 'For the rest of the time that the shows are here, all the rides to you are free.' I cuddled him and said thanks. There and then he took me and Cathie down to his fairground, and we went on every ride for free. That was one of the best times of my life when I was small, and before they left the showground, Mrs Taylor bought me proper earrings to go in my pierced ears.

We stayed in my granny's house for another year, then got a house of our own in Macdonald Crescent, a housing scheme in Blairgowrie. When we moved there I never went out much, as I was frightened the other kids would hit me. We stayed in that house for two years then moved to another house in the same scheme.

While we were there, the Second World War broke out, and my father had to go away to France to fight. I never understood then why people had to fight in wars. All I knew, and hated, was that my father had to be away from us.

While I was a child I can't remember us ever having the house to ourselves, as we always had people staying with us. My first real friend was a girl named Marlene Mitchell. Her father, Ace, her mother, Mickey, and Marlene all stayed with us for many years, until Ace went to the war with my father.

Then Mickey's sister, Gladys, came to stay with us, and that was when all the trouble started. Men started coming to the house to see Gladys, but she only brought them in when my mother wasn't around. All hell broke loose when, one day, a relative of the family came to pay Gladys a visit. I was curious about what went on up the stairs when the men arrived, so I sneaked up to the bedroom door and I could hear that they were grunting like pigs. I was shocked and very frightened.

When my mother came home, she found me crying at the foot of the stairs. I couldn't speak, but just pointed upstairs.

My mother ran up and went into the bedroom. First to come down was the relative. He was carrying his jacket and pulling his braces up over his shoulders, with a look of guilt and shock on his face. This was followed by Gladys tumbling down as my mother pushed her and her belongings down the stairs. My mother opened the front door and pushed Gladys out with her things on to the pavement, shouting all the time words that I didn't know existed. I didn't ask what they meant because my mother was too angry to answer.

That was the last time we saw Gladys, or dirty Gladys as my mother called her after that. Looking back on this scene, I believe that it marked my first introduction to sex.

My father and Ace came home on leave after that, and Ace told Mickey off for allowing her sister into the house in the first place.

My mother allowed Marlene and Mickey to stay, but that didn't last long. After my father and Ace went off to Dunkirk, Mickey herself started inviting men back to the house. Of course my mother put her and Marlene out, and they moved to Montrose to stay with Gladys. We never saw any of them again, and I missed my best and only pal.

2
School and Wartime

❧

I was about five when my uncle Donald took me under his wing to teach me songs and ballads. The first one he taught me was 'If I Was a Blackbird'. At that time he said it was his favourite song.

Even now, when I sing it, I hear his voice in mine, it is there even in the pronunciation of the words. It took me about a week to learn it, sitting on his knee and getting it by heart the oral way. This is how the song goes:

Chorus
Now, if I was a blackbird, I'd whistle and sing,
And I'd follow the ship that my true love sails in,
And on the top rigging I would there build my nest,
And I'd flutter my wings on his lily-white breast.

Now my parents they chide me and will not agree,
That me and my sailor boy married should be.
But let them deprive me and do what they will,
While there's breath in my body, he's the one I love still.

Chorus

Now if I could meet him, I would bow, I would kneel,
And if I could meet him, I would bow to his heel.
I would tell him my sorrow, my grief and my pain,
Just since he's gaed and left me in yon flowery glen.

Chorus

My mother was overjoyed that I had finally learned a ballad from my uncle Donald. Many more followed, one after the other. I remember one day my mother made a deal with my uncle. She would teach me the ballads, and he would teach me how to sing them properly the traveller's way.

Not long afterwards I started at the Rattray primary school. I have written my memory of this in an earlier book of mine, *Pilgrims of the Mist*, and I will tell it again here. When I was six years old, my mother and father said to me, 'You must go to school, and learn to read and write like other bairns'. So when the school started up after the summer holidays I was put to school.

I was a very shy child when I was six, and terrified on my first day. How would I be able to cope with spending time among the country hantle (non-travellers), me being a traveller? I had never done it before. I had always been within the security blanket of my family. What was going to happen to me now?

In a state of panic, I held on tight to my mother's hand all the way down to the school. When we entered the school gates there were more kids than I had ever seen in my life before. So I crawled under my mother's coat like I used to do when it was cold in the winter. My mother hardly noticed what I was doing, as she was used to me doing it.

We went into the school through the front door, and were told to wait and see the headmaster, a Mr Douglas. After about ten minutes, we were ushered into his office by the school secretary, a dour-faced woman.

'Well,' said the headmaster, 'you want your child to go to this school?'

'Yes, I do,' said my mother, 'if it is alright with you.' I burst out laughing. My mother used to make up little rhymes, and each line included the initial of someone's name. I said to her to complete the rhyme: 'Somebody H is thinking of you'. At home we played games like this all the time. The headmaster glowered down into my small impish face. 'Well, we have a fine one here, a joker no less. We will soon put that nonsense out of you, my girl. You can go now,' he said to my mother, 'I will take her to her class.'

My mother kissed me and told me to behave, not to cry, to do what I was told, and off she went. Mr Douglas took me by the hand to my class. He dragged me along as if I was a dog on a leash.

I went into the classroom and a smiling teacher greeted me with a cuddle. The headmaster said to the teacher, 'Don't stand any nonsense from this one. She is one of the tinker clan, you know, and a bit of a joker, I believe.'

'She will be fine with me, sir,' said the teacher, and I was never so happy as when I saw Mr Douglas close the door behind him. I got another cuddle from the teacher, and all my fears went away.

At playtime I was standing by myself in the playground eating a bit of toast my mother had made for me that morning. I got pushed from the back and fell to the ground clutching my toast. A foot came down and stood on my hand with the toast in it, trampling my fingers and the toast into the ground.

I let out a yell, but soon stopped, remembering my granny's words: 'The country hantle are always right, because they have the education, and we don't.' I was brought up this way, to think I must have done something wrong that deserved punishment, and it was my fault that this had happened to me.

So I said nothing, and washed the mud off my hands, to make sure that the teacher wouldn't ask me what had happened. 'The traveller is always wrong and they are always right,' I kept saying to myself all day.

When bell-time came, I ran home as fast as I could. My sister was waiting for me at the school gate. Was I glad to see her, you bet I was. I never mentioned to anyone what had happened that day at school.

If someone was to ask me what were the worst memories of my life, it would be school, especially that first day.

For many days to follow, every evening I was pounced on by this same girl, who was called Morag. She was three times my size. The other children called her baby elephant. She used to lock me in the toilets and beat me up every evening. She would send me notes in class: 'You are a TINK, and don't you forget it, scum'. She used to sing to me:

'Tinky, tinky, torin bags,
Awa tae the well and wash yer rags!'

Then she would slap me across the face, and she always stuck her own big fat face in mine. I remember saying to myself, if there ever was an ogre, she was one of them.

A few days later she was off school. She must have been ill or something, and I was so happy not to be tormented for those few days at least.

While she was away, there was a new rule announced at school. We children would run and hang on the back of the milk van when the milk was delivered at playtime. The rule was that we were not allowed to do it any more.

However, Morag being off school didn't know this, so she jumped on the back of the van. She was sent for by the headmaster. He took her into her class, and using his double-thong belt, he strapped her in front of all the pupils in the room. I felt sorry for her, but not too sorry. I remembered my granny's words at that time, 'God's no sleeping'. Were her words coming true, and was he protecting me?

One day Morag ripped the clothes off me, and sent me home in my knickers. I was mortified. She said I had been wearing her frock. How could I? I weighed about four stone, and she weighed about ten stone.

Her father owned a fruit shop. She used to bring rotten fruit to the school, and pelt all the kids in the yard with it.

One day she was caught kissing a boy behind a shed at school. The other children said they were 'fumbling'. At the time I didn't know what that meant. She was sent home with a note from the headmaster, and was off school for a week.

A few of the children got together and decided that when she came back we were going to do something about her bullying. I said I wanted nothing to do with it. So they left me out of it, but agreed that I could watch. That suited me fine. There were three boys and two girls that she always gave a hard time to. They went into the toilets, the boys in theirs, and the girls in theirs. The girls peed in a can, and the boys shit in a paper, and they waited and waited in one of the toilets all crushed together. I was waiting outside. She made a remark to me, but I have forgotten what it was, and went into the toilet. After about five minutes I heard this unearthly scream. The gang came out of the toilets so fast they nearly knocked me down. Then Morag came flying out, covered in pee and with shit running down her face.

At that very moment a teacher came round the corner, and saw her. The rest of us were chasing each other and playing away as if nothing had happened.

The teacher nearly took a fit when she saw her, and the smell was terrible. 'Who did this to you?' the teacher demanded.

'I don't know, miss, I never saw their faces.'

I can tell you, she still bullied us at school afterwards, but not so much. It was me she picked on the most. She blamed me for things I hadn't done. Then she went and told the teachers. I got the belt once while I was there. She plugged newspapers down the toilet and said I had done it. The headmaster sent for me, and I got the two-thong belt double-handed. I never felt pain like that in my life.

When he told me to go back to my class, I ran home. Once my father saw the state of my hands, he took me with him and marched right into the headmaster's office. I was standing there terrified. My father grabbed the headmaster by the collar, took his two fingers and poked them into his eyes. 'Will that fit you?' he said.

I was tortured at the school till I was twelve. Cathie, my sister, tried to help me, but they did the same to her. No matter how we tried we never made any friends. I am so glad my cousin was there, we were inseparable growing up.

Then I moved to the High School. I liked that a lot better.

Any travellers reading this will know what I went through

at that time. I am now an old woman, yet that memory will be with me forever.

One day I was coming home with my brother Andy. We took a shortcut home by the Putting Green, and we had to cross over a fence. Andy helped me over, then let go of my hands and I fell onto my knees. What we hadn't seen was a broken bottle hidden in the grass, and I got a deep gash on my knee. When I got home it was only Cathie who was in the house. She bandaged my knee and put oil of silk on it to keep the bandage from sticking. Then she put me to bed and pampered me till my mother came home.

That year we went camping up to Aberfeldy. It was a great haunt of ours. We called it the family Wagon Train, as so many of us went up there. We stayed on a farmer's field for two weeks, then came home. It was great, we could wander anywhere we liked, the freedom was unbelievable.

At night people would tell stories round the fire. I will never forget the first time my granny, father's mother, told me a story. It has been my favourite one ever since I first heard it. One night my granny shouted to me and the rest of the kids who were there, and said she had a story for us. I was having my supper and couldn't go there and then, but my mother said, 'take your plate with you, lassie.' So off I went. When I got there, everybody was round the fire waiting for me, because my granny wouldn't start without me being there. Here is the story she told.

Aippley and Orangey

There was once this man whose wife had died, and he was left to bring up his wee lassie on his own. For a pet name he called her Aippley, and he adored her. A year later he met a woman who also had a wee girl, and he married her. He called her wee girl Orangey for a pet name, though she was really called Jeannie.

Now the woman hated wee Aippley, because her father loved her so much, but Orangey liked wee Aippley, and they always played together. The father worked in a mill in the town and was away all day, and never saw how the wife treated his daughter. She made her do everything in the house, and wouldn't let Orangey help her even though she wanted to.

One day the mother shouted to wee Aippley to go an errand for her. 'Aippley, I want you to go to the dairy to get me some milk.'

Now, Aippley had always admired the jug that her stepmother and her father had been given as a wedding present, and she asked if she could take it to the dairy for the milk. The mother thought, then said, 'Well, you can take it, but if anything happens to it, you're dead, my girl — do you hear me, dead.'

'I will guard it with my life, mammy, honest I will,' said wee Aippley.

So off she went to the dairy and got the milk, but coming out of the door of the dairy, she tripped and fell, and the jug smashed to smithereens.

She was panicking so much she sat down and cried, and was afraid to go home, when a gentleman passed and asked her why she was crying. So she told him the whole story.

'Never mind, my dear, come with me and I will buy you a new jug. Your mother can't be that bad.' So he took her to the hardware store and bought her a new jug, and filled it up with milk as well. Off she went home after thanking the man very kindly.

When she got home, her stepmother was in the garden hanging out washing, so Aippley put the jug on the table with the change and went and hid. The stepmother came in, looked at the jug and started to scream Aippley's name. 'AIPPLEY, AIPPLEY!' she shouted in her loudest voice, and both girls came running.'

'Where is my jug?'

'I can explain,' said Aippley, and she started to say what had happened when her stepmother stopped her.

'What did I say I would do if you broke my jug?'

'That you would kill me.'

'Orangey, go down to the shed at the bottom of the garden, and in there you will find an axe. Bring it to me!'

Orangey hesitated, but her mother shouted at her to do what she was told. She fled out the back to fetch the axe.

After putting a pot of water on the fire to make soup, the woman took Aippley out into the back garden. She laid wee Aippley on a block, lifted the axe and cut her up into small pieces. She put the flesh into the pot, then she told wee Orangey to take the bones and bury them down at the bottom of the garden. Orangey dug a hole and buried them.

The mother boiled up the bits of wee Aippley in the pot, and said to wee Orangey, 'She will make a fine pot o' soup for your father's supper when he comes home.'

When the father came home he shouted for wee Aippley to say he was home.

'Och, never mind her. Just now I have made a fine pot o' broath for your supper. Sit down at the table and eat.'

The father lifted up his spoon and took some broth in it, and there on the spoon was wee Aippley's finger wearing the ring he had bought her for her birthday. He threw it down and started to scream, 'Aippley, my wee Aippley!' Then he collapsed and fell to the floor.

A few days passed and he thought, 'What can I do about it, now my wee Aippley is deed and gone?'

Well, time went on till a few days before Christmas. In the father came one night and said to his wife, 'Have you seen that doo-doo [white dove] flying round our chimney and our house? It has been here for a few days.'

'Yes, I did notice it,' said his wife.

Now, the night before Christmas, the wee doo-doo left the house and went up to the main street where all the shops were open late for Christmas Eve. It flew up the street till it came to a large jeweller's shop, and fluttered in through the door and landed on the counter. It said to the owner behind the counter, 'If you give me a man's pocket-watch from your shop, I will sing you a wee song.'

Startled, the man said, 'Doo, if you sing me a wee song you can have the best pocket-watch in my shop.'

The doo-doo started to sing:

> My mammy killed me,
> My daddy ate me,
> My sister Jeannie picked my bones,
> And put them atween two marble stones,
> And I growed into a bonny wee doo-doo.

The man was so pleased the doo had sung to him that he gave it the best pocket-watch in his shop.

Then off the bird flew further up the street till it came to a toy shop. It fluttered in the door, landed on the counter and said to the shopkeeper, 'If you give me the biggest doll you have in the shop, I will sing you a wee song.'

'Oh my God, Doo, if you sing me a wee song I will gladly give you the biggest doll in the shop.'

The doo-doo started to sing:

> My mammy killed me,
> My daddy ate me,
> My sister Jeannie picked my bones,
> And put them atween two marble stones,
> And I growed into a bonny wee doo-doo.

Off again the bird flew till it came to a big hardware shop. It fluttered in the door, landed on the counter and said to the shopman, 'If you give me the biggest axe you have in the shop, I will sing you a song.'

'If you can sing to me, Doo, you can have anything in my shop.'

So the bird sang:

> My mammy killed me,
> My daddy ate me,
> My sister Jeannie picked my bones,

And put them atween two marble stones,
And I growed into a bonny wee doo-doo.

The doo-doo got the biggest, sharpest axe in the shop, and off it flew back to the house where the man and his wife stayed. It landed on the chimney and shouted down: 'Daddy, are you there? It's me, wee Aippley. I am up the chimney. Hold out your hands, I have a present for you.'

'Oh, my wee Aippley, I am here, darling.' He went to the fire, held out his hands and down came the pocket-watch.

'Is Orangey there?'

'Aye,' she shouted. She held out her hands and down came the big doll.

'Is my mammy there?' asked the doo-doo.

The stepmother ran to the chimney and looked up. And the wee doo dropped the axe and cut the her head off, and it fell into the pot of water that was boiling on the fire.

That's the end of my story. My granny said it was a very ancient story. It will always be my favourite.

It was wartime now, a frightening few years for us.

We were in bed one night when the air-raid siren went off, and a hard knock came to our door. It was the blackout warden to tell us German troops had landed just outside Blairgowrie at Loch Bog, and that we had to go to the shelter at the Davie Park until we heard the all-clear. We girls were terrified, but my brothers, Andy and John, thought it was great.

We made our way to the shelter with our gasmasks on – mine was a Mickey Mouse one with a floppy nose – and crawled into the entrance. The shelter was pitch dark, and half-full of folk. A few of them were drunk and were singing.

Ten minutes after we arrived, a fight broke out and all the women were screaming. Two men were arguing about who was going to win the war, us or the Jerries (that's what we called the Germans). I was sitting not too far away from them when something wet hit me in the face and trickled down. One of the men ran out of the shelter and fled, while the other man groaned and then went quiet.

We sat terrified until we heard the siren go for the all-clear. Just then the warden came in, shone his torch at us and gasped. Sitting beside me was the man who had been fighting earlier. He was staring up at the ceiling, eyes bulging out of his head, and as stiff as a doornail. He had a big knife sticking out of his chest, and on my face was his blood that had splattered on my cheek.

We all got out of there as quick as we could. I heard a few days later that they couldn't find the man who had done the stabbing, and they never did. It took me and my family a long time to get over the man being killed in the shelter, and we never went back to it — we hid under our bed from then on. There were no more air-raid shelters for us.

Things that happened to us during the war were terrible. With all the rationing we didn't have enough to eat, and we had hardly any money. We only had what my father gave my mother from his army pension, which was seven shillings and sixpence in old money (37p), per week. My uncle Donald helped us out a lot then.

My father had come home from Dunkirk shell-shocked, and half the man he was when he went away. My mother and father's bed was in the living room of our house, and I remember coming down one day when I heard a great commotion going on down the stairs. When I went into the living room, Ace Mitchell and my mother and a few other folk were tying my father down on the bed, and were waiting on the doctor coming. The doctor arrived with an ambulance in tow, and they took my father away bellowing and screaming. I remember crying hard as I saw my father being led away to the ambulance, and wondering what was going on. All I could do was cry.

My mother got all us kids together round the fire and told us my father was very ill, and had to be taken away to hospital. My brother John asked my mother why. She said, 'It was fighting in the war that made him ill, and the noise of the guns did something to his mind. All he needs is rest.' We were very sad that night, and I remember that was the first time I can remember asking God to make my daddy well again.

My father was put into a military hospital at Larbert. That was where all shell-shocked soldiers went that came back from the war. I remember the first time my mother took me down to the hospital to see my daddy. I was so shocked at all the soldiers walking about talking to themselves. One man jumped up from where he was sitting and scratched his head, and I remember I said to my daddy, 'That man has an idea.' I went over to him before my father or mother could stop me and asked him what his idea was. He just smiled and danced off as if he was a ballet dancer. I was more confused than ever.

My father was in the hospital for four months. I remember the day he came home. He was quiet and didn't say very much. He just stared blankly all the time.

He came out of it quite soon, though, with us speaking our own language, the cant, to him in our own way. He still had a lot of nightmares, and used to wake up dripping with sweat about three times a week. It took him a long, long time to be himself again, if he ever was. I was too young to remember what he was like before he went away to war.

Not long after, my mother fell pregnant. She went to Meikleour House near Blairgowrie to have the baby. They had to open this as a maternity hospital because there were so many babies being born as a result of the Polish soldiers being billeted in the area. The local maternity nurses couldn't cope.

My mother had a wee girl, but it only lived half an hour. Some of the people in there said that when the midwife was bathing the baby she slipped out of her hands and hit her head on the side of the sink, but we don't know for sure. What a tragedy that was in our life.

A year later, my mother fell pregnant again. I won't go into detail, but the child was still-born. A few weeks later my mother and father adopted a wee girl, who was the pride of our life. We got her when she was ten days old. I got to name her, and I chose the name Rena. I was no longer the boss of the household, Rena was, and that suited us all just fine. The joy she gave to us is indescribable.

My sister that lived half an hour was buried in a proper grave in Rattray churchyard, but the still-born baby was buried without a gravestone in the same graveyard, up against the wall. She was buried after dark with no minister, only the grave-digger and my father.

3
After the War

❧

I was eight when my father bought me a bike, and every night the family came with me across to the Davie Park to teach me how to ride it. After many, many skinned knees and scraped elbows I finally got the hang of it, to the delight of my family. They were getting fed up of taking me there every night.

One Sunday two of my cousins came through from Montrose. We went for a walk down the Loon Braes, which was a special haunt for all the kids in Rattray. It was a gorse-ridden place with a small swamp where we could fish for frog-spawn and play hide and seek. This particular Sunday, about three o'clock, we heard something rustling in the bushes, and voices. We went very quiet and sneaked up closer. There was a woman there who started to make the worst noises, and a man was there grunting so hard it frightened us. The woman was shouting 'Oh no, oh no!' We thought the man was murdering her. The three of us grabbed sticks, or whatever was at hand, and attacked the man, hitting him with all our force. He jumped up and ran away, pulling up his trousers. We went over to the woman with big grins on our faces, thinking we would get a thank you from her, but she screamed and swore at us and chased us away. We didn't know then what we had done wrong, but the woman did.

It was a hard life then, with my father not long out of the army. He was still suffering from the war, and us being travellers he couldn't easily find employment. He had a bike and used to go up the glens to the farms to catch rabbits and collect the rabbit skins. He got sixpence each for them, and that helped.

I can always remember the work we did for the farmers when I was aged about ten. By this time my father had a small car, and we had moved from the council house to a yard in Old Rattray. My father had bought a two-bedroomed hut, and rented the land from Hill Whitson of Parkhill.

There was an old derelict building on the land. Downstairs was completely gutted, except for the staircase, but upstairs was a bedroom. My father went up to Dunkeld and got my grand-father's brother Duncan and his wife to come and live in the room. The two of them moved in and were so happy at being taken out of a bow tent and to be near family.

A few days after they moved in, my uncle Duncan went with my father to look for farmwork. I crept up the stairs to Bell, my father's auntie and my grand-aunt.

'Come in, my lassie, and give your auld auntie a cuddle.' She was a lovely woman, but the smell of tobacco off her would choke a gruffy (pig). At these times I took a big breath and held it till I got my cuddle.

'Now,' she said, 'Have you any old newspapers or books I could have?'

'I will soon get you some, auntie. I will be back in a minute.'

Down the road a bit there was a berry field next to a house, which belonged to the old gravedigger, William Hovelrood. He had a shed in which he collected newspapers and magazines. It was chock-a-block with every kind of paper and book. I knocked on the door of his house and asked him if I could have some. He gave me as many as I could carry, and I took them back to the auld wa' stanes, as we called the derelict building where my aunt and uncle stayed.

I hurried up the stairs to my auntie with all the papers.

'Auntie, what do you want them for?'

'You will soon see, my lassie.'

She moved what furniture she had – a bed, two easy chairs and a table – to the centre of the room. Then she said to me, 'Does your mother have any flour meal?'

'Oh, I am sure she has.'

I ran off to get some, still puzzled by what she was going to do with the papers, or the flour meal.

When I came back to her, she had a half-full basin of water ready, and a stick in her hand. She poured the flour into the water till it was thick, stirred it round, and started to put it on pages from the newspapers and magazines. Then she stuck them on the walls. 'I have to paper my walls with something, and it will be lovely when it is finished,' she said.

She papered the walls with the most brightly coloured pictures from the magazines, and when she had used up all the magazines, she started on the newspapers.

Neither she nor my uncle Duncan could read or write, but she put the pages the right way up, and said my father and mother could read them. I was amazed at the beauty of the colours.

We moved all the furniture back again, and sat and admired her work. She was so proud of it she cried, and hugged me again. I forgot to hold my breath this time, and I got the full force of her smell.

By this time, my father had an old Ford lorry that he used for collecting scrap. I remember one day he was selling some to a scrap merchant. The scrap merchant was another traveller, and he always bought our scrap. He told my father there was a panic of some kind among travellers who were staying up north a wee bit, and he thought my father should go to try and calm things down.

So we got ready, and on the Sunday we went to where they were camping. There would be about twelve families there, all camped at the side of a wood. We pulled in with my father's lorry and they all came out to greet us. Some of them were crying, and we wondered what in the name of God was the matter with everyone.

A man ran up to the lorry as my father got out and said, 'Oh, Alex, come wi' me.'

We went with him, and he made us sit at his fire, where

everyone else was gathered. Then he said to his wife, Maggie, 'Get them.'

First came a boy in a buggy pushed by his father. Then a woman came with two girls, one on each hand. All three were deformed. They were small and very bow-legged.

'Alex, what is wrong wi' the wains?'

'Well,' said my father. 'The bairns have rickets.'

He explained what rickets was, that it was caused by the lack of calcium and there was no cure.

'Does that mean the bairns will stay like this?' said one of the women.

'Yes,' my father said.

There was a sadness went through the tents.

One of the men asked if we would stay the night, because the kids wanted my father to tell them stories. We decided to sleep in the back of our lorry.

So we all sat round the big fire. They gave us blankets and we got ready for the stories.

A wee boy came up to my father and said, 'Alec, can I tell my story first?'

'Aye,' my father told him, 'of course.'

Another man chimed in and said, 'Me first, Ronnie boy, and you efter me.' So the man told this story.

'It was my father that told me this story,' he said.

The Baker Boy

There was a man away up in the north of Scotland, and he was like a hypnotist, he could do all the tricks of the day. He was called the Baker Boy, and he went round the fairs and markets when my father was a wee laddie.

An old woman had been out of the town to cut some corn for her goat. As she came back in through the market, she had two sheaves of corn on her back.

All the folk in the market were in a big crowd round the Baker Boy. He was standing in the centre of the ring, and he was calling on them all to come to see the cock that could pull a lerrick (larch) tree. The folk all crowded round, and they saw the cock pulling a young lerrick tree with its beak, tossing it about and pulling it about.

The old woman came in at the back of the crowd and said, 'What are youse looking at?'

'Oh, you never saw anything like this, missus. It was a cock pulling a lerrick tree.'

She pushed past a man that was blocking her view and went to have a look.

'That's no' a lerrick tree,' she said, 'that's a corn straw!'

The Baker Boy turned to the old woman quick, and said, 'I'll tell you what I will do, old woman. I will give you a guinea for those two sheaves of corn to feed my cockerel.'

She said, 'A guinea? Oh, but I will give you them for that.'

She gave him the two sheaves of corn, and then when she looked down again, she made sure to tell everybody she could see the cock pulling the lerrick tree!

One day the Baker Boy was in Campbeltown, and there he met a traveller man called Curly Donald, because he had ringlets right down to his shoulders. He was a very hardy man, he stood over six feet.

When he met the Baker Boy, he said, 'Hello there, Baker, I see you're in the toon the day.' He knew the Baker Boy would be there so he could go round the fairs.

'Oh aye,' said the Baker Boy, 'I will have to try and earn some money the day. You look a bit haggard, Donald. Have you been on the booze?'

'Aye,' said Donald. 'I have drunk myself oot. I dinnae have a penny to get myself a glass o' beer.'

'Och,' said the Baker Boy, 'here's half a croon to you. Awa' and get your beer.'

So in Curly Donald went to the pub and said to the publican, 'A half o' whisky and a glass o' beer.' The publican put the drinks in front of Donald. He grabbed the whisky and downed it in one, and he was just reaching for the beer when the publican said, 'Hi, Donald, what are you playing at, this is no' half a croon.'

'Oh aye, it's half a croon, alright.'

'No it's no', Donald. Look at it, it's a roon' piece o' leather, man.'

The controversy got up and there was an argument, and the publican sent for Sergeant Cauley.

Now the Baker Boy was standing drinking at the bar all this time and laughing.

Sergeant Cauley came in and said, 'What's wrong, MacInnes?'

'Och,' said the publican, 'Donald here has called for a drink, and to pay for it he is trying to palm me off with a round piece o' leather.'

'Let me see it,' said the policeman. The publican lifted it from the back of the bar.

'Look,' he said, 'you cannae buy drink with that.'

The sergeant took it from him and looked at it.

'But that's alright – it's half a crown.'

The publican said again, 'It's not half a crown, it's a piece o' leather.'

'Now,' said the policeman, 'I will give you one of my half-crowns and I'll keep this one, and that's the argument finished.'

He turned round, put the publican's coin in his pocket, took out one of his own half-crowns and gave it to MacInnes.

As the policeman left the pub, the publican noticed the Baker Boy standing there against the bar, laughing.

'Oh,' said the publican, 'I might have known! Come on, Baker, you'd better get ootside, and do your mesmerising some place else.'

The Baker Boy went away with a big smile on his face. He had won again.

'Come on now, Alec, it's your turn. This is what the wains are waiting for, your story.'

My father told a story he hadn't told for a long time.

The Three Feathers

Once upon a time there was a king who lived in a castle away in the far parts of the country. He had three sons, and one day he came out and called his three sons to a turret high up in the castle. He said to them, 'Sons, I'm getting very old now, and I won't have long to live. I must give you each a task to do to see which one I should leave the castle to.'

'What kind of task will it be, father?' asked the oldest son.

'The one that brings me back the best tablecloth will get the castle.'

'That will not be hard to do. Which way will we go to look for the tablecloths?'

'Well, I will give you three feathers,' said the king. 'Each of you will throw one up in the air, and whichever direction it goes, that is the way you will follow to look for your tablecloth.'

So, next morning, the three sons went up to the top of the turret, and the king handed them a feather each.

'Now, throw your feathers up to see which way you are going to go,' he said.

So the eldest son threw his feather up, and it went south. The second son threw his up, and it went east. The third son's feather went down behind the castle.

The father laughed. 'You won't get much of a tablecloth down there, Jack,' he said, still laughing. 'Oh well,' said Jack 'I can't help it.'

The other sons set off to look for their cloths, but Jack waited and waited, till eventually his father came to him and said, 'You only have three days left to go and look for the tablecloth, Jack.'

'Oh well, I will go round and see where my feather has landed, father.'

He went round to the back of the castle, and he found his feather sitting on the top of a big stone with an iron ring on it. So he lifted the feather and put it in his pocket, then lifted the big stone by the ring. Underneath there was a dark hole and steps going down, and who was sitting at the bottom of the steps, but a giant frog.

'My goodness, Jack, you haven't given us much time to get you the tablecloth.'

'Oh, you can speak!' said Jack.

'Yes, I can speak,' said the frog.

'No, I admit I haven't given you much time to get me a tablecloth.'

'Never mind, Jack. You come in and have something to eat and drink, and I will have something to give you when you leave.'

So Jack went down the steps and had his food and drink, and it was a lot of wee frogs who were serving him.

When he was going out, the big frog handed him a parcel.

'Here you are, Jack,' he said. 'Now don't open it till you're in front of your father.'

Jack said to himself, 'This can't be much of a tablecloth, the parcel is so small.' He went home.

The next morning the oldest brother came back with his tablecloth. It was a real silk one, and it was beautiful.

'That's a lovely tablecloth,' said the king.

The second brother came back, and his tablecloth was the same as the oldest brother's, but a different colour.

Then Jack came wandering up. 'Are these the two tablecloths you have got?' Jack asked.

'Yes, that's the two tablecloths,' his brothers said.

Jack put his hand in his pocket and pulled out his wee parcel. His father laughed. 'By the size of that wee package, that can be no bigger than a handkerchief,' he said.

'It doesn't matter,' said Jack. 'You open it.'

So the king opened the parcel, and there was a silk tablecloth fringed with gold all round.

'Oh, I have never seen a tablecloth like it Jack, never in my life,' said the king. 'You have won, Jack.'

Jack was surprised, but his two brothers protested, 'That's not fair, we want another chance.'

The king looked at them and said, 'Alright, I will give you three tasks altogether. The second one is to see who can bring me back the best ring, the bonniest and most expensive one.'

So next morning they went up to the turret again, threw their feathers in the air, and one went north, and another one went east, but Jack's feather again went down the back of the castle.

'Well, I know where I got the tablecloth,' said Jack, 'but getting a gold ring may be more than the frog can do. Anyway, I will try.'

So he went to the stone, took hold of the ring and pulled it up, and went down the steps again. There was the big frog in front of him.

'Well, I suppose you will know why I am here?' said Jack.

'Yes,' said the frog, 'you want a ring. But never you mind, come in and get something to eat and drink, and I will see what I can do.'

So Jack went and got something to eat and drink, and the wee frogs served him. This time there was dancing and a band playing music. The frogs were playing fiddles and accordions and all sorts of instruments. Jack had a good time there. He stayed all night, and the next morning the frog came and handed Jack a wee box. 'Now, don't look at it till you are in front of your father, and let him open the box.'

Jack put the box in his pocket and up the stairs he went.

Next, it was up to the castle turret. The two brothers were already there, and each of them had a gold and diamond ring.

'What did you get, Jack?' asked his father. 'It won't be much of a ring you got down the back of the castle.'

Jack handed his father the box, and when he opened it, the sparkle dazzled his eyes. It was a beautiful ring with diamonds and nuggets of gold.

'Oh,' said the king, 'I have never, ever seen a ring as pretty as that, Jack. You have won again.'

The two brothers were angry and said, 'We will try to beat him next time.'

So next morning they went up to the turret and threw their feathers again, and they all flew off in the same way as before. Jack's feather went down the back of the castle again.

'Now, this time,' said the king, 'you will look for a bride.'

Jack thought to himself, 'I'll go down tonight and see the talking frog, but I don't want a frog for a wife.'

So off he went to the back of the castle. He took the iron ring in his hand, lifted up the stone and went down the steps.

The frog said, 'Come down and get something to eat, and I will see what I can do for you.'

After Jack had all he wanted to eat and drink, the frog came back. 'Jack,' he said, 'you go up the steps and do what I tell you.'

When Jack went up the steps, there was a carriage and pair waiting for him, sitting in the driveway up to the castle.

The big frog gave him a wee frog, and told Jack to put it on the seat of the carriage. When he did so, it turned into a princess. She was a real beauty. As soon as Jack sat in the carriage beside her, his clothes changed into a marvellous suit that was fit for a nobleman.

When they drove into the courtyard of the castle, the king realised it was Jack in the carriage. The other brothers had not returned. When the king looked in the carriage and saw the princess, he was amazed how beautiful she was. This time he gave Jack the castle, and he and the princess lived there happily ever after.

4
Working on the Land

❧

I often think about the different kinds of work we did when I was growing up. Six weeks of the year, from the second week in July till the end of August, we went raspberry-picking. We got up at 5 a.m. every weekday to get a bucket at Parkhill Farm. We had to queue for our buckets when it was still dark, and then we were told which field to go pick in. It could be the Switchback, the Fishers Mayer, or the Vaults. In those days farmers gave their fields names, but not now.

It was a hard job, raspberry-picking. You had to pick as fast as you could, because it was piecework, and your hands got all scratched. The pickers were paid a halfpenny per pound. My father always said it was slave labour, but we had to do it to survive.

The raspberries on the farm were called Norfolk Giants. I was only eight-and-a-half, and the gaffer wouldn't let me pick because I couldn't reach the top ones, so I played about the field all day.

A year or two later we were at the berries again. One evening we were sitting round a camp-fire at Cleves berryfield on the road to Essenday. The other berry-pickers asked my mother to tell a story, and here is the one she told.

The Girl and the Devil

This is a story about a woman and her man who stayed in a wee house not far from the village, maybe about half a mile down the road.

They had one daughter who wouldn't go out. She always

stayed at home. She cleaned the house, and did all the work in the house, but she wouldn't go out.

So about dinner-time one Saturday, her father said to her, 'Mary, why don't you ever go down to the village and see if you can't find a boyfriend or something like that?'

'Oh, I don't want to go down to the village,' she replied.

'But this is Saturday,' her father said. 'Why not go to the dance tonight? There is a dance every Saturday night in the village.'

'Oh,' said Mary, 'I can't dance at all.'

'Well, you can always learn,' her father said.

At about five o'clock that day, Mary came in and said, 'I think I will go to the dance tonight after all, father.'

'Yes,' he said. 'Go to the dance tonight.'

So off she went to the dance. It was in full swing, and everyone was dancing, but she went and sat down.

A young man came across to her and said, 'Why are you not dancing?'

'Oh,' Mary said, 'I am sorry, but I can't dance.'

'Anyone can dance if they put their mind to it. Just try, I am sure you can do it.'

So she got up, and he took hold of her, and she danced away.

'I told you you could dance. You are dancing splendidly,' said the young man.

Well, they danced the whole night through, and when the dance had finished, he said to her, 'Can I take you home?'

'I don't mind,' she said.

So the two of them walked up to the house where she stayed. He took her right to the gate, and they said goodnight.

'What about next Saturday night, will you be down at the dance?'

'Oh, I think I may take a run down to the dance again,' said Mary.

The young man said, 'Be sure of it, because I will be there.'

So a week went past, and Mary got herself all dressed up and went down to the dance again. The young man was there, and they danced for the whole night again.

In the early morning he said, 'Will I take you home again, Mary?'

'I don't mind,' she replied.

So the two of them walked slowly up the road, and he said to her, 'Have you ever had a boyfriend before?'

'No,' she replied, 'I have never had a boyfriend.'

'Well, what about me?'

Mary replied, 'I really don't know.'

'Oh, you know fine,' he said. 'I have never had a girlfriend before either. So why don't we join up together? Then we might get married.'

'I don't know,' was her reply. 'I will tell you next Saturday at the dance.'

So the next Saturday came and Mary went away down to the dance. She was sitting down at the side of the room and in came the young man. He went up to her and said, 'Well, have you made up your mind?'

'I will tell you after the dance,' she said.

The two of them danced all night together, and at the end of the night he said, 'I will take you home now.'

So they walked right up to the gate of the house.

'Are you going to marry me?' he asked.

'Yes, I will marry you.'

'Oh, that's fine,' said he. 'You will have to wait for a year, and then I will come back and claim you. I will be away for a year, and when I come back I will call on you.'

However, when he was turning away she happened to look down and see his feet, and he had cloven hooves. The young man was the Devil.

Mary didn't know what to do. She went into the house, and she worried all night. The next day she couldn't do anything for worrying. She thought to herself, I have promised myself to the Devil!

Her father recognised from her quietness that something was troubling her and said, 'What's wrong with you, have you fallen out with your boyfriend?'

'No, I haven't,' she said. Then she told him the whole story.

'Oh, my goodness. You'd better go down and see the priest.'

So she went away down to see the priest, and she told him everything.

'That's terrible,' said the priest. 'But don't worry, my dear. When are you going to see him again?'

'He is coming back for me in a year's time.'

'Well, in a year's time, don't stay in your own house. Come down here to me.'

'Alright,' she said.

So time rolled by till the year was up. She was still going to the dances, but she didn't see the young man again.

When the year was up, she went down to the priest's house.

'Oh, is the year up?' asked the priest.

'Yes, it is,' she said.

'Well, we had better go away down to the chapel. When is he going to call for you?'

'He is coming for me about six o'clock at night.'

'He's coming at six? We had better get down to the chapel at once.'

So they went away down to the chapel. The priest stood right in the middle of the floor, and he put holy water in a circle round the two of them. He stood there reading the holy Bible.

Six o'clock came and they heard a knock on the chapel door. The priest shouted, 'Who's there?'

'It's me,' replied the Devil. 'I have come for my wife.'

The priest paid no attention, he just kept reading his bible.

The knock on the door came louder. 'I have come for my wife!'

The priest replied, 'If you put your hand in my hand, you can have your wife.'

But the Devil couldn't put his hand in a holy man's hand.

'No, I will not, but I must get my wife at once!'

The Devil gave a deafening roar, and the chapel shook and shook.

'Come in, then,' said the priest, 'come in. If you are a man at all you will come in for her.'

The Devil threw the door open, but just stood there, he couldn't come in. Then he went up in a puff of smoke. So that was the end of the Devil, the priest had won.

Mary lived a happy life after that.

After the berry-picking came the potato-lifting. We always went to a farm at Blacklaw, four miles from Blairgowrie. Everybody had to pick a stretch of the field called a bit, measured out by the foreman. It was five shillings a day for half a bit, which a child would do. Cathie did a full bit and got ten shillings a day.

Then came harvesting: flax, which makes linseed oil, corn, wheat and barley. We pulled the flax out of the ground by hand, which was a lot easier than other harvesting, because flax is a surface crop and the least thing pulls it out of the ground. There was a flax mill in Blairgowrie that made the linseed oil. My father scythed the corn, wheat and barley, and the woman and children tied it and stooked it. That was very hard work. We were paid by the acre from the farmer, and my father went to the same farms every year.

Then there was neep-shawin – turnip-harvesting. That was a cold, dirty job. I have seen my father having to kick the turnips out of the ground. One year, two days before Christmas, we had no money, but my father had got a turnip field from the farmer to shaw the week before. He said to my mother, 'Belle, I will have to go and try to shaw some of these neeps, because we haven't a penny.'

'Well,' said my mother, 'If you are going, so are we.'

We all bundled into the back of the lorry: John, Cathie, Andy, myself and Rena. We just got to the field when the snow came on, and it was bitterly cold. We tried to get the neeps out of the ground, but they wouldn't budge.

The farmer, Mr Shanks, was coming down from the farm and stopped when he saw us in the field. He came striding over to us, and we were like snowmen.

'Alex, what the hell are you doing, man, on a day li

'Well, must is a good master,' said my father. 'We haven
penny to our name, and it's near Christmas.'

'Well, well,' said Mr Shanks, 'stop right there. I will pay you
for two rows now, and you can do them after the new year.'
(A row was four drills at 120 yards long, and he paid us for two
rows, so that was eight drills.)

The money he gave us lasted us till after the new year, and on
the third of January we were back in the field paying the farmer
back for all his kindness.

I remember one year me and Cathie went to Blacklaw to
gather the tatties. Coming home at night on the back of the
tractor, a girl opened her mouth and started to sing. She hadn't
a great voice, but the song was wonderful. I learned it before I
got home that day, and all on the back of a tractor. My uncle
Donald always said you never know where you will hear a song.
Here is the song she sang that day:

> A man came home from work one night
> And found his home without a light,
> He went upstairs to go to bed,
> When a sudden thought came to his head.
>
> He went into his daughter's room,
> And found her hanging from a beam,
> He got his knife and cut her down,
> And on her breast these words he found:
>
> 'Oh dig my grave, and dig it deep,
> And put white lilies at my feet,
> And at my head just place a dove,
> To certify I died of love.'
>
> So all you maidens bear in mind,
> A soldier's love is hard to find,
> But if you find one good and true,
> Don't change the old love for the new.

5
Leaving School

✿

Life went on as usual. We worked with the farmers, collected scrap and rags, and went pearl fishing.

I was nearly twelve when I went up to the High School in Blairgowrie. That's when the bullying stopped, much to my relief.

I loved the High School. We weren't treated as if we were ignorant kids there. The teachers were great. I was taken out of class often to sit for the pupils in their art class, and I got the job of being registration girl, taking the register twice a day. I was in heaven. I loved it. I thought all the bullying was over. Little did I know what was to come.

One day I was out playing in the playground when a tall girl came over to me and pushed me down so hard, I had burn marks on my knee. 'You evil girl, you,' she said, 'You are taking my Albert away from me. He told me last night he was finished with me and wanted someone else. When I asked him who, he said it was you.'

'I can assure you, you are mistaken. I don't even know the boy.'

'He said you would say that. You slut, moving in on my boy-friend. You're dead!' She made a dive at me again and punched me on the nose, and the blood gushed out of it. I panicked, and headed for my register teacher.

The teacher sent for the girl and the boy, and he admitted he had named me, to protect his new girlfriend from the old one. In front of the teacher he said, 'She is only a tink, anyway, and can stand a beating.'

I told my brother Andy that night when I got home, and he was waiting for the boy coming out of school the next night. I pointed him out and Andy grabbed him by the collar. He said into his face, 'Now, wee man, I am going to give you a tinker's beating,' and he did. The boy never bothered me after that, and things got back to normal at the school. I was never picked on again all the time I was there.

We went up the following weekend to see Frank and Ruby. They were my mother and father's best pals, and every now and again we would go up to Banff for the weekend. We had great ceilidhs up there.

That weekend was the first time I fell in love. It was with a traveller boy who was staying on the shore in their caravan for the summer. We kissed twice and that was as far as our love went – we were too young to think of getting up to bad things.

When we were there we paid a visit to Duff House. This was before they did it up, and it was derelict at the time. There were four of us prowling from room to room. We were walking through a dark passage, when we heard the rustle of skirts and someone passed us in the corridor like a puff of wind. Well, we started to panic, and scuttled up the stairs and out the front door as if the Devil himself was after us, never to return again to Duff House.

That night my mother and father and Frank and Ruby had a wee drink in their house, and the singing started. Ruby's mother was there, a great old lady, and by God, she could sing. Ruby herself had a deep, lovely voice, we had never heard a woman with such a rich singing voice. That was the first time Ruby sang to us her version of 'Red Roses'. This is how it went.

On the banks of red roses my love and I sat down,
And he took out his charm box to play his love a tune,
In the middle of the tune, his love broke down and cried,
'Oh my Johnnie, lovely Johnnie, dinna leave me.'

He took oot his pocket knife, and it being long and sharp,
And he pierced it through and through his bonny lassie's
heart,
And he pierced it through and through his bonny lassie's
heart,
And he left her lying low among red roses.

That was all Ruby could sing, as she was getting the worse
for wear with the drink.

Then my mother sang while Frank played the piano, and by
God, could he play the piano. He played in a way that, no matter
who you were, it could stir you, all heavy pipe tunes. Then my
dad played the pipes. But guess what I did? I sneaked out the
door, not wanting to sing, and went to play kick the can.

The next morning, Frank's brother, who stayed with their
mother, auld Maggie, came running into the house gasping for
breath, and all shaking and panicky. 'Oh my God, oh my God!'
he kept repeating to himself, over and over.

Frank grabbed him and made him sit down. He told him to
keep calm, and tell us what was wrong. When he was as calm
as he was going to get, he said, 'I found a dead body on the
beach, a man's body. I was looking through his pockets and
came across all this money – there was thousands of pounds in
his pocket.'

Frank gasped. 'What did you do wi' it?' he asked.

'But wait,' said his brother. 'There were heaps of cheques in
his pockets as well.'

'OK, OK,' said Frank. 'But what did you do wi' it, man?'

'I ran to the police station and told them, and handed all the
money to them. They are down there just now, and the beach
is sealed off.'

Frank shook his head, but patted his brother on the back. I
couldn't make out what was going through Frank's head at that
moment, but he was in deep thought.

Frank and my father had a walk down to the beach to see
what was going on. The chief of police came up to Frank and

said, 'That's a great brother you have there. As honest as the day is long.'

'Aye, he is that,' said Frank, and the policeman shook Frank's hand.

Later that night, about ten o'clock, Frank's brother came in, all smiles.

'What are you so happy about?' asked Frank.

His brother put his hand in his pocket, pulled out a wad of notes, and threw it on the table.

'I ken you think I am daft, but I am no' that daft to hand all the money in. That's your share, Frank.' Frank got £1,000.

After a few years they still hadn't found out who the dead man was, so Frank's brother got all the rest of the money, because he had been the one to find it. He was a happy man.

About a month later I was down in the town of Blairgowrie with my cousin when a boy approached me. He was one of the better class of boys in the town, and I had caught him looking at me a lot when he met me. He asked me if I would go to the pictures with him the next night. I was thrilled, and said yes, I would love to go.

Next night I met him in front of the cinema. Even now I can remember the name of the picture – it was *The Seven Deadly Sins*. What it was about I don't know to this day. He didn't hold my hand or put his arm around me, which I was glad about. I would have been mortified if he had. He took me home after the film, and by this time I was in agony for a pee. I couldn't bear for him to see me go to a toilet. We stood outside my house (well, the hut we lived in at the time) and he kissed me twice. He said goodnight very politely, and away he went, looking back all the time as he was going down the road.

I was in seventh heaven that a boy from the other side of the tracks could ask me on a date. It was the first date I had been on.

About eight the next morning, I got up and went outside to the spot where he had left me the night before, and lying on the path was eight half-crowns. I wondered where they had come from. I picked them up and looked at them, then put them in my pocket.

I went down the town a few hours later, and met this girl who was one of the local in-crowd. As she approached she was laughing.

'Well,' she said, 'did you enjoy your night out yesterday, at the pictures?'

Innocently I replied, 'Yes, thank you.'

She burst out laughing again. 'You did know he did it for a bet, don't you? We all gave him half-a-crown each to take you. There were eight half-crowns.'

Then the penny dropped, and I put my hand in my pocket and took the coins out.

'Is this what you are talking about? Yes, he told me, and he gave me these.'

You should have seen her face. She didn't know I was lying through my teeth. I kept the money and enjoyed spending it. Why he threw them away has always been a mystery to me. I never spoke to him again. My poor heart was broken, but I survived.

That weekend my father said we were going up to Banff again, but I said I didn't want to go, so I stayed behind with my uncle Donald. The rest of the family went away on the Friday, and my uncle Donald and my brother John took me with them to the car sale in Forfar. By this time my uncle was teaching my brother John how to deal in second-hand cars. We arrived at the sale about six-thirty. We always went early to view the cars before they went through the sale.

One of the dealers came up to my uncle Donald. 'Hi there, Don. I have something you may be interested in buying.' He took us out of the sale-ground and showed us a horse. It was a big garron, pure black with a white mane and black tail, a lovely horse.

When my uncle saw it he fell in love with it, I could tell, but I knew there was no way he would buy it. He felt its legs and all its body, but kept very quiet, which wasn't like him. He turned to the man and said, 'I'm not interested, sorry,' and walked away. We followed him back into the sale.

He bought nothing that night. On the way home, John said to him, 'You are very quiet, Uncle, what's wrong with you? You haven't said a word since we left the sale.'

'That was an evil horse that the man was trying to sell me. I recognised it. It killed a man and his wife just a month ago, stamped them to death.' Then he just shook his head, and nothing more was said about that horse.

When my mother and father came home from Banff that week, they came in the door not speaking. Then the argument started. When my mother and father argued it was ferocious. From the age of about nine I used to hide down at the bottom of our garden among the bushes, with my fingers in my ears so that I wouldn't hear them. Periodically I would take my fingers out and listen to see if I could hear shouting, and if I did my fingers would be stuffed back in my ears. I used to hum to block out the noise. I was terrified of them arguing.

That time I must have sat there for two hours. It was just as well it was summer, or I would have been frozen. Things finally calmed down, and when I went up to the house my mother was in her bed, things were broken and Cathie was cleaning up. I always remember the sigh of relief when it was all over. Arguments like this would happen about twice a month.

The year now was 1950. I was 15, had left school, and went with my father most days hawking. One very hot day we went up the glen to go to some farms in Glen Isla. My father was collecting fleece wool, rags and maybe some scrap. Anyway, my father was dying for a cup of tea. He usually got tea from one of the farms, but this day he noticed some smoke in the distance in a wee wood. My father said, 'There's travellers, we will get tea fae them.'

So over we went to where the smoke was coming from, and sure enough there was a wee bow tent at the side of this wee wood, and an old man was sitting at the fire waiting for his can to boil, smoking his pipe.

'God bless my soul, Alex, is that you?' he said when he saw us.

'Aye,' said my father, 'it is that,' and he sat on the ground beside the old man. 'What are you doing here, man, all by yourself? I thought you were up biding at Aberfeldy.'

'Aye, I was, but I got chased oot by a few travellers for being cheeky. You ken what I am like when I get a peeve [drink].'

'Where's Mary, your wife?' asked my father.

'Och, I left her wi' her mither, she will be fine.'

The old man made a cup of tea. It was about the best cup of tea I had had for a long time: very strong, sweet, with plenty of milk in it, and the main thing was, it was stewed. Travellers are used to stewed tea. My granny made a big kettle of tea every morning. She added a quarter of tea, a pound of sugar and a pint of milk, and it lay at the side of the fire stewing away, and anyone that came in got a cup of it.

My father got up to go and I stood up as well.

'Will you be back the morn, Alex?'

'Yes,' said my father. 'I have some scrap to collect fae a farm near here.'

'Fine,' said the old man. 'Could you bring me up some baccy? Black Bogie roll.'

'I will,' said my father. The auld man offered him the money, but my father wouldn't take it.

The next day my father got a phone call from a farmer in Pitlochry about some scrap. The farmer was going away and needed it shifted. So my father never got back with the old man's baccy that day. We went up the next day instead.

When we got there, all was quiet as we approached the tent. The tent was still as it was before, but there was no sign of the old man.

My father found him in the wood, lying dead with a bundle of sticks in his arms. He had taken a massive heart attack. My father told me then what the old man's name was, Alex Stewart, and that he was a cousin to my father.

We left after covering him up, and phoned the doctor, but he wouldn't come. He said he would look at him if we brought him down to his surgery in Alyth. We went back to the old man, and my father gathered him up in his arms, carried him out of the wood and put him in the back of our lorry.

The doctor in Alyth pronounced him dead. He had died of natural causes, the doctor said. 'Now what do you expect me to do with him? Take him to his wife and tell her to deal with it.'

So my poor father had to load him back into the lorry and take him up to his wife Mary in Aberfeldy. He was buried in Kenmore. All my family attended the funeral. My father gave Mary the Black Bogie roll.

6
Making Ends Meet

It was now getting very difficult for my father to make both ends meet. One day after teatime we were all sitting round the fire when he said to my mother, 'Belle, times are getting hard. After the harvest, we will have to think of a gimmick to make enough money to see us through the winter.' My mother's eyes lit up – she loved a challenge, did my mother.

A few days later, the potato-picking started. We were in the field gathering tatties when my mother shouted to my father that she wanted a pen and paper. Grudgingly, he said he had none, but eventually gave her a pen. He said he had no paper, and threw an empty cigarette packet on her lap, saying, 'That's all the paper I have got.' She smiled, and said 'That will dae.'

Then she started to write, giving a wee laugh now and again at the words she was putting down. 'Alex, this is going to be the gimmick of all gimmicks, mark my words.'

Using what she wrote, she made what we called bills to put through people's letterboxes asking for rags, woollens, old clothes and scrap, anything they were throwing out. She made two different bills six months apart. My goodness, they did the trick. Here is the first one.

Dear madam, I'm calling your district today,
For your old cast-off clothing I'm willing to pay,
Your old rags and woollens, I'll just do the same,
Believe me, dear madam, I'm new at the game.

You may have been cheated in days that's gone by,
But it won't cost you anything to give me a try,

And if I can't please you, there's no harm done,
Believe me, I know, there are crooks on the run.

They give you a few pence for the clothes that you wear,
They know they have cheated, but what do they care,
And someday, no doubt, they'll retire with a pile,
But honestly speaking, that isn't my style.

I like to be honest with all whom I meet,
The rich man, the poor man, the tramp on the street,
And if I make a living and keep my way clear,
I won't make a fortune when I pass on from here.

Here is the second bill:

Dear madam, I'm calling your district today,
When you pick up my card, please don't throw it away,
Just you sit down and read it, you never can tell,
You may have some old junk that you want to sell.

Perhaps an old mattress, or maybe some brass,
For old stuff like that is far better in cash,
You may have some jewellery you no longer like,
Or a second-hand car, or your husband's old bike.

Your old rags and woollens are of no further use,
I am sure they are far better oot o' the hoose,
And your old cast-off clothing, your ain or your man's,
Your old iron pots, or your brass jelly pans.

They are the things that I'm after, tae mention a few,
So get up and get busy, gie the hoose a guid do,
And you'll no be sorry when I call to collect,
I'm the first honest dealer that you've ever met.

We put the bills out in the morning, and on them we said we
would call back in two hours. These bills of my mother were

an instant success. My father got a better lorry out of the money he saved up.

There were a lot of travellers who used to go round collecting our cards and the stuff that was meant for us. We caught them at it and they never did it again.

That year, at the berry time, we heard that my father's cousin, Jeannie Robertson, with her husband Donald and his brother Isaac, were down at the berries at the Brig of Ruthven, so we paid them a visit as we always did.

We arrived at her camp about two o'clock on Sunday. There was a commotion going on as we went in there, and everyone was laughing like mad. My father went up to Isaac. 'What's going on here?' he asked him.

'Oh, hello, Alex. We are just having a bit o' a laugh with Eddie here.'

We sat at the fire and Jeannie told us about Eddie. They were calling him the mole-catcher. Jeannie could hardly tell us for laughing. 'Well, Alex, Robbie fae the next camp said he would give Eddie a pound for every mole he could catch by hand. Eddie, God love him, is a wee bit simple, and the next field is overrun wi' moles. Eddie has been telling us what he is going to do with all the money he is going to make as a mole-catcher. Now, as you know, Alex, the only way to get moles is to gas them out o' the holes. But Eddie doesn't ken that.'

Then Isaac chimed in. 'Yesterday he was all day waiting for the moles to come out of their holes. He was chapping [knocking] on the mole mounds, as if he was knocking on their doors, and that's what we are laughing at.'

After Jeannie had fed us, which she always did, she said, 'Let's have a ceilidh roon the fire.'

The men got a big fire going, and sitting round with cups of tea, and the rest of the travellers over from the other camps, we started with songs. Jeannie sang one of her beautiful ballads. What a voice Jeannie had, she was one of my favourite singers, and always will be. To me there was only one Jeannie Robertson, and no one could come close to her.

'Come on, Alex, it's your turn now. Give us one of your stories,' said Jeannie.

'Right,' said my father, 'here's one. The name of it is "The Shepherd's Misfortune".'

This is a story about a shepherd who was getting married. He stayed with his father and mother in a house in the country. He said to his father, 'Father, tomorrow's the day I'm getting married.'

'That'll be all right,' says the old man.

So the next night, after he had got married, they had a great big celebration. The dancing and playing music was all in the shepherd's house.

Then the old man came over to his son and said, 'Listen, son, it's only about eleven o'clock and the drink's all finished. What are we going to do?'

'Oh, I'll tell you what we're going to do,' says the son. 'It's only about three miles to the pub. I'll go and tell the man that the drink's all finished and I'll get a puckle bottles o' beer and some whisky.'

His father said, 'Will ye manage it noo?'

'Oh, I'll manage it all right,' said the son. 'Give me my stick, my cromach stick, and my shawl and I'll get going.'

So he got his stick and his plaid, and he threw the plaid over his shoulder and set off down the road. But before he went away, his father said to him, 'Now listen, son, if you meet anything on the road, don't touch it, and don't say a word to it. Just you march on and never mind it.'

'Oh, that's all right,' said the son, 'I'll not speak to anything. What would I see on that road anyway?'

His father said, 'You never know. You might see something.'

So he set off on the road and he marched on this road until he had to go across a wee bridge. He was crossing over this bridge, and there was something just went 'wheecht!' right by his neck and pulled the muffler off him.

'My goodness,' he said, 'What was that? My muffler's gone

anyway, I ken that. Something pulled it off my neck, but I cannae look for it the noo, I must go on or I'll be late for the pub.'

So he went on to the hotel, he rapped at the door and he got his drink. Then he came back over the bridge again and right up to the house.

And he said, 'There's the drink, Father.'

'Oh, so you got it?' said his father. The son replied, 'Aye, I got it all right.'

So after they're drinking and dancing away, this young shepherd man, he's sitting at the fire and he's getting drowsy and drowsy and drowsy. His father came over and said, 'There's something wrong with you, son. What's wrong?'

And his son said, 'I cannae tell you, Father.'

'Did you meet anything on the road when you were going for the whisky and the beer?' asked his father.

'No, I never met anything, but something flew past my head and took away the muffler off my neck.'

His father asked, 'Did you not get the muffler back?'

'No,' replied his son.

'Well, you'd better go back and get that muffler at once,' his father replied.

His son said, 'Where's my stick?'

'You'd better not take that stick with you,' said the father, 'because if you do, it'll maybe turn out worse.'

But his son replied, 'Give me my stick, Father.' So he got the stick.

Finally his father said, 'Don't touch it, whatever it is – don't touch it!'

So the young shepherd went away back along the road now, and back along the road, till he came to the wee bridge. It was a bright moonlit night. He looked over the bridge and he heard something crying, 'Eeh, hee, hee! Eeh, hee, hee!'

'My goodness,' said the young man, 'What's that?'

He went down to the water's edge and he looked and he saw a wee woman, just an old fairy woman, and she was sitting at the burnside washing his muffler. And she was washing it and washing it and washing it.

'Oh,' said the shepherd, 'It was you who took my muffler from round my neck, was it? You're the one that took it. You'd better give it to me.' And he put his hand down and plucked it from her.

'I'll mak' sure you won't take a muffler from another man,' he said. So he spat on his stick and he gave three wallops at this wee woman at the burnside, and the wee woman was roaring, and she was jumping, and he never touched her. He couldn't hit her, for she was jumping about six or seven feet in the air. So he got tired laying into this wee woman and he went away home.

'Well, did you get your muffler back?' his father asked.

The son replied, 'Aye, I have it in my pocket, there it is.'

So his father looked at it, and he held it between him and the lamp on the mantelpiece, and he looked and he saw that it was threadbare. 'It's threadbare!' he said. 'If the muffler had been worn right through, there would have been a hole in your heart and you would have died. She would have rubbed a hole in your heart.' He said, 'I hope you didn't touch her.'

'Oh, no,' said his son, 'I never touched her, I only gave her three or four whacks with this stick.'

'Laddie,' his father said, 'you shouldn't have touched her. She will haunt you all the days of your life.'

So, oh, a week passed and the shepherd and his young wife were sitting at the fireside. The shepherd was taking his supper about six or seven o'clock at night and a rap came to the door. So the woman went out to see what it was but, ah, there was nobody there. She couldn't see anybody, so she went back in and sat down again. Again a rap came to the door.

'Wait a minute,' the shepherd said to his young wife, 'I'll go out this time.'

He went to the door and there was the wee woman. 'Here, shepherd,' she said, 'you are to fight me, one hour a night, for one year.'

'Fight you?' he said. 'Nobody could fight you, you're ower wee.'

'Ah, but,' she said, 'I'm a wee woman the noo, but wait a minute till I turn myself into my right form. Then you'll see wha I am.' So she turned herself, and then it was the Devil, and he was standing at the door.

'Come on, shepherd,' the Devil said, 'me and you must have a fight for one hour every night for a year.' So the shepherd was fighting the Devil and fighting the Devil, and oh, he came in half bended down, sore and bruised, and his face all cut.

'My goodness!' his wife said, 'What happened?'

'Oh, nothing at all,' said the shepherd. 'I must have fallen down.'

So for about three months the same thing happened every night. Eventually he spoke to his father and said, 'I cannae stand it any longer, Father.'

'I told you not to meddle with thon wee woman. You shouldn't have touched her. The best thing you can do now is to pack up and go to America, and the Devil won't know where you are.'

So the shepherd packed up and went away to America, and he was on the boat one night on the deck, and there in front of him stood the Devil. 'You needn't try to get away to America, shepherd. You have to fight me for one hour every night.'

So the two of them started fighting and fighting on the deck.

Then the captain of the ship came down and said, 'What are you doing, shepherd?' He couldn't see the Devil, but he could see the shepherd battering away at something.

When the shepherd landed in America, he thought to himself, 'There's no use staying here. I'll have to go back home again. No matter where I go he will be there.' So he came home again.

And the shepherd fought the Devil for a year and a day, and on the last night, the Devil said to him, 'Now, this is our last night, shepherd, and it will be the hardest night of the lot. I must say you're a hardy man, shepherd, yes, a hardy man.'

So they started to fight, and fight, and fight, and at the end of it the shepherd was crawling on his hands and knees home. 'Wife,' he said, 'I'm about done. I'm finished, put me to bed.' So he went to bed, and he lay for three days.

After three days, the nurse and the doctor arrived. 'What happened to you?' asked the doctor.

The shepherd replied, 'I am sorry, doctor, I can't tell you.'

'You're bruised all over,' said the doctor. 'You're black and blue, but I will give you some kind of an ointment to rub on you all over, and we'll see if it will do any good.'

The shepherd took the ointment and rubbed it all over himself, but it was no good. It didn't make a bit of difference to the pain.

On the Sunday night a knock came to the door. The shepherd's wife went out, and there stood the wee woman. 'I hear your husband is in his bed,' she said.

'Yes he is.'

'Could I come in and see him?'

'Yes, come in,' replied the wife.

The wee woman went into the house and saw the shepherd. He looked at her and said, 'You're back again.'

'Yes, but I am not here to do you any harm, I am here to cure you.'

'How can you cure me?' asked the shepherd.

'Well, sit up a minute.'

So he sat up. She took her hands and rubbed them all over his back, and the same on his front, and his face, and legs, and arms, and hands.

'Now get up and get your clothes on. I am away now and you will never see me again. I'm away!' And she flew out the door.

The shepherd got up and started to dance round the room. 'She has cured me! That was the woman I had to fight every night, and now she has cured me!'

And that's the end of my story.

Now it was my mother's turn to do something.

'I'm no' going to sing the night. Alex put me in the mood for a story, so I am going to tell you "The Dear Child". It's no' a long story. It's aboot something that happened by Loch Ordie, near Riechip and Ramore. They say "Bonny Riechip and bonny Ramore, are two bonny places I'll never see more". Loch Ordie was a place we used to pick larch cones away back.

It was at one of them shooting gatherings the gentry have. A servant girl got in tow with one of the gentlemen, and she fell with child. When she was expecting, her mother and father cast her out, and wanted nothing more to do with her.

She had a child, a wee girl, and managed to hide her till she was about two months old, when the time for the shooting party came round again. She told the gentleman about the baby, and he would take nothing to do with her. So she used to keep the child well hidden from the big house, where she worked as a servant.

The child lived deep in the forest on her own in a small hut the mother had found. The servant girl used to go back and forward to see that the child was alright. This went on till she was old enough to run around.

After a while the servant girl got fed up looking after the child, and the secrecy surrounding her, so one morning she just packed up and left the child, her job, everything, and cleared out.

The wee girl was left running wild, living with the deer of the forest. This went on for a number of years, and the child ran around with the beasts of the forest, and hair grew all over her body, because she never had any clothes to wear.

Now there was a party out shooting on the hill one day, and they saw the child running in front of them. They had never seen anything like it in their lives. They kent it wasn't a deer, or a beast, so they chased the child and caught her. They took her back with them. She couldn't speak or anything. The girl's mother was never found. The gentry kept the child and brought her up, and later she became Lady Ardvorlich. So that is the story of the deer child.'

(That was a story my granny told my mother, and she swore it was the God's truth.)

'Belle, that was a great story,' said Jeannie.

'Well, we will have to go now, Jeannie,' said my father, 'but we have enjoyed oursels. When are you going hame?'

'Oh, no' for another two weeks yet, I think.'

'Well, cheerio just now,' said my father, and off we went home.

That was the time the gypsy family came and stayed in our back garden. My father had met them at a fair in Ireland the year before, and invited them to come to see us and pick raspberries. The day after we paid Jeannie a visit, a knock came to the door, and standing there was a man and woman dressed in the most beautiful clothes I had ever seen, and there was jewellery dripping off them.

My father came to the door, and excitedly let them in. Only the man and his son could speak any English. The mother and the girl were draped in veils that covered their faces, but when the tea arrived they took them off and, oh my God, they were beautiful women. Their skin was light chocolate-brown, with not a blemish.

I don't remember their names, but the son's name in English was Stanley. Their surname, I will always remember, was Mutaravich.

The old man didn't pick berries. He had a big dancing bear, and went through the towns letting folk see it. In Blairgowrie, people took its photo and it is still there today, the photo I mean.

We went with the others to show them how to pick berries, and I partnered Stanley. He was gey slow at picking the berries, and I asked him why he was taking so long. 'Sheila, I am dying for a smoke and haven't any cigarettes. My mother and father don't know I smoke, and they would not approve of it. What am I going to do?'

'Well, my father is not here so I can't get anything from him. Have you got a cigarette paper?'

'Yes, but nothing to put in it,' said Stanley.

'Give it here to me,' I said. I took some withered berry leaves, crushed them in my hand and rolled them in the fag paper. When Stanley smoked it, a huge smile came over his face and a look of calm. 'Now I smoke berry tobacco,' he joked, and he laughed heartily.

A few days later he told me he had to go back to India, as it was time for him to collect his wife. The marriage had been arranged years before. So off he went. I was excited for him. He was away for over a week, and came back with a small skinny girl, who was supposed to be 16, but to me looked about 13. She was pretty girl, but with not a picking of flesh about her body.

They had been married in India when Stanley arrived there, but we had a celebration when they came back. The mother danced and so did the daughter, and Stanley's wife sang. She said it was a song about leaving her homeland. They didn't drink much – Stanley and his father had a few glasses of beer, but the women only drank tea.

They stayed till the end of the berries, and they would have been good company if the women had spoken English, even a wee bit.

The day they were leaving, we helped them to pack up. They said they would come back, but the old man died, and they never did return. I will never forget the Mutaraviches. I have always been intrigued with their name, I think it is beautiful. That was my first introduction to gypsy people, and it was a great experience.

7

Auntie Bella

❧

One of the great people in my life was my auntie Bella, my
father's sister. What a great storyteller she was. I don't want to
miss her out. Here, in her own words, is a story she told me.

The Wild Man of Dunkeld

Many years ago, my grandmother said to me, when we were
going through Dunkeld woods, 'There's a well over there in
that part of the wood. Have you ever seen it?'

'No, granny, I never saw it.'

'Well,' she said, pointing to a patch of bushes, 'it's over there
somewhere.'

I looked where she was pointing and said, 'There's nothing
much there.'

'Oh, but wait till you hear about the well!' she said. 'You
don't know the history of that well, do you?'

'No, granny, I don't.'

Then she told me the story.

Long, long ago, in these woods there lived a hairy man. He was
wild, covered all over with hair, and he couldn't speak, he only
squealed out of him.

He ran about the mountains and through the woods, and the
police and the authorities tried to capture him, but he ran as fast
as a hare and he was always too quick for them.

However, they knew that very often he came to this well for
a drink of the water. So the police and the authorities decided
to run the water out of the well, and put whisky in it instead.

In those days whisky was of no value and it was not expensive to fill up the well.

For the next few nights they watched and waited for him to come to the well. Eventually, after dark, the wild man of the woods came to drink the water.

When he tasted it, he started laughing to himself, and he was overjoyed with the taste. He was down on his elbows with his head in the well. He had no cup, so he just stuck his head down and lapped up the whisky, and he drank, and drank, and drank.

First he tried to get up, and was staggering all over the place. Then he collapsed and fell asleep.

The authorities were able to capture him then, and they put him away in a house away up about Amulree called the Hermitage. The wild man stayed there for years and years until he died.

I remember one night we were at my auntie Bella's house. Maurice Fleming, the folk-song collector, was going down to record her the next day, and she had us down to ask us if the song she had picked to record would be suitable for him. Then she and my father started squabbling as usual. He said the song she had chosen was horrible, and we said she could sing what she liked.

After a while the squabbling stopped, and she asked my father if he was hungry, as she had a pot full of gruffies' tramplers (pigs' feet). She must have had about a dozen in the pot. She couped them into a basin, took them to my father and the two of them ate the lot.

The rest of the family never would eat them, but my father always did. I remember what he said to auntie Bella before she brought them through, 'I hope you shaved them first.'

'Don't speak about shaving! I ruined Billie's razor wi' the damn things, and he made murder wi' me.'

Have you ever eaten pigs' feet? They are so sticky that your fingers get glued together. Auntie Bella and my father were making jokes about the stickiness, and laughing their heads off.

After the merriment and laughter had died down, my father said to her, 'Now, Bella, let us hear that horrible song you are going to sing.'

Well, didn't she take the huff at him. 'Alex, you are nothing but a fool. Now hold your tongue, because no matter what you say, I am going to sing this song to Maurice,' – and she did.

Kilmarnock Town

In Kilmarnock town there lived a maid,
She was handsome, young and fair,
She was courted by a false young man,
That drove her to despair.

Now nine long months had passed and gone,
This maid began to mourn,
Saying, 'Willie, will you marry me
Before my baby's born?'

'To marry you it's a thing I shan't,
Nor I never intend to do,
So go away home, let your parents know
What Willie has said to you.'

'To go home and let my parents know
Would bring to them disgrace,
So I'd rather go and drown myself
In some dark and lonely place.'

So Mary put on her lily-white robe,
Her body to destroy,
And kneeling down she kissed her child,
And said, 'Farewell, my boy.'

Onc day as Willie was walking,
Down by the banks of Clyde,
Oh there he spies his Mary-Ann,
Coming floating with the tide.

So he lifted up her lily-white hand,
To see if life was there,
And he cried, 'God bless you, Mary-Ann,
You should have been my bride.'

My auntie Bella loved this song my mother always sang,
maybe because Bell was who it was all about:

Betsy Bell

Oh, my name is Betsy Bell,
In the Overgate I dwell,
Nae doot you'll wonder what I'm doing here,
But if you wait a wee,
It's my tale I'll tell to ye,
A tale nae doot you'll think it's very queer.

For I'm lookin for a lad,
And he may be good or bad,
I'm going to take the first yin that I see,
He may be young or auld,
Or grey-heeded, fringed or bald,
It's onything that wears the breeks for me.

Chorus
Oh, but of lads I've had my share,
And I've haen a score or mair,
But hoo they threw me up I dinnae ken,
But I'm neither prood nor shy,
That the lads should pass me by,
I wonder what's adae wi' a' the men.

Noo as I gaed oot last nicht,
Sure, I met wee Sandy Richt,
And he hauled me in as I was passin' by,
And he asked me if I'd wed,

And this is what I said,
'Man, if you are quite agreeable, so am I.'

Noo I was so prood of the chance,
Sure wi' joy it made me dance,
The merriage it was to be right there and then,
But when I got my merriage frock,
Ach, he said it was all a joke,
So I wonder what's adae wi' a' the men.

Chorus

Noo as I gaed oot yestreen,
I could scarcely believe my een,
For I saw auld Janet Cook wi' a lad,
And if it's true what folk say,
She'll be wed a month the day,
Man, the thocht's enough to drive a body mad.

Now I ken auld Janet Cook,
And she drinks just like a juke,
And her age it runs aboot three score and ten,
And it's for husbands she's had three,
And there's no' a chance for me,
Oh, I wonder what's adae wi' a' the men.

Chorus

But if there's ony laddie here
That would like a little dear,
A widower or a bachelor though he be,
If on merriage he is bent,
I will gie him my consent,
It's no' every day he'll get a chance like me.

For I can weave and I can work,
I can wash and mend a sark,

I'm as thrifty as ony lass I ken.
But on the nail I'll hing,
And I'll aye get leave to sing,
I wonder what's adae wi' a' the men.

Chorus

8

Hotel Work

❧

At the age of 16 my life changed forever. One day I said to my mother and father that I was fed up working in the fields and hawking the houses, and that I wanted a change. By this time my brother Andy had raspberry fields, as did my father. I worked long and hard with Andy, planting the berries, chatting them (cleaning the weeds away with a hoe), cutting them out and lacing them (tying them up). I had had enough. My parents were alright with my decision, but my uncle Donald said to me, 'Where are you going to get a job, lassie, in this town? You ken you're a traveller, and have no chance.'

'Well, I can only try,' I said.

Next day I went down to the town and approached people at one of the hotels. It had been taken over by new owners, and I got a job as a waitress. They didn't know who I was, and believe me, I never told them. My wages were three pounds, three shillings a week, for many, many hours work, but I loved it. It was a very busy hotel, and I felt proud to work there. It showed me how the other half lived, because it was a posh hotel. I was dressed in black with a stiff plastic collar, plastic cuffs and a waitress's hat. I looked great.

After I had worked there for a month, I was finishing my shift very late every night. One night I noticed a car following me. It was going very, very slowly behind me, all the way home. The car never stopped near me, it just followed me as I walked. This went on night after night, and after a while I got very frightened. One night I approached the car, and asked the man behind the wheel what he was doing, following me every night. He said, 'I mean no harm, I just want to see you home safe.'

I had mixed feelings about this, and decided to let him carry on, as he meant no harm. During the day, when I saw him in a shop, he was very courteous and tipped his hat to me. I found out he was Polish. Gradually I began to feel safe about him and wasn't frightened to walk up the road any more.

I may say I turned a few men's heads when I was young. I was a looker. I was very innocent about everything, and it showed.

One night there was a concert party booked into the hotel. They were to appear at the town hall the next night, so they were booked in for a few days to do rehearsals. That was when I met the famous Will Starr, an ace accordionist, and what a man he was. Little did I know back then I would be on the stage one day myself. Will Starr spoke all the time about his mother, he loved her so much. He was not a man looking for a woman, and I was glad about that. He was my pal, more than I can say about the rest of the cast. I got free tickets to see the show, but of course I was working, and had to give them away.

The hotel accommodated many well-known artistes and public figures in the year I was there. One Saturday night we had a big party of politicians in for a conference. They had their dinner and a lot of booze. I was in the kitchen and was asked to go upstairs with coffee for one of the guests. When I got to the staircase one of the politicians was with a woman on the stairs and was having sex with her. I ran back to the kitchen and sat down. The chef asked me how come I was looking so pale. I could only point to the door.

He went out to see what was happening, then came back and spoke to me. 'Now, Sheila, that is a very important man in politics, and the woman he is with is not his wife, so you must keep this to yourself. Alright?'

I nodded, but little did I know that the couple had spotted me running away. Next morning at breakfast the politician was sitting with his wife, and the woman sat with her husband. I served them, but I couldn't look at them.

After they left, I was called into the office by the owner of the hotel. She handed me an envelope and then sent me away. I was puzzled. I opened the envelope in the staff room and found £20 in it. I thought to myself that this was money for me to keep quiet about what I had seen. I wasn't too happy about it, but I gave the chef half of the money, and spent the rest on my mother, getting new pots and pans and a tea-set.

On Braemar Day in September, a big day in the Blairgowrie calendar, the hotels were usually chock-a-block, especially for lunchtime and high teas. This year there were a lot of folk for lunch, passing through on the way to the Highland games.

An old lady came in with her chauffeur. Her driver went to the kitchen to be fed, and I showed the dainty old lady a seat in the downstairs dining room. She didn't look well, and I said to her, 'Are you alright, madam?'

'No,' she said, 'I have a terrible headache, and that is why I stopped here for lunch, to see if it would settle.'

We were so busy that day I was run off my feet, but I went to the kitchen and got two aspirins and a drink of water for her.

'Oh my dear, you're so busy, and you take time off to get me something for my headache!' she exclaimed.

'I can't let you suffer, madam, if I can help at all.'

That evening I wasn't on duty. I was exhausted after doing all the lunches and breakfasts, but then I got a phone call from the hotel. Could I come back down, as I was wanted.

So down I went, and there was the old lady, asking me if I would go to England with her as her companion. I said I would have to ask my parents, so her driver drove me home, and of course my mother and father said no. She went away a very disappointed lady. My mother said to me, 'If you go you might not be heard of ever again.' I was glad I was staying after that.

That Christmas, me and my cousin went to our first dance in the town hall. My mother and father didn't know I was going. The dance was on Christmas Eve, and we were so excited about it. We went to Perth to buy new dresses for it.

We arrived at the dance, and half way through the evening a man came up to me and said, 'You are number eight.' What he meant I didn't know.

An hour later, the girls with numbers were called to the stage. It was a 'Miss Christmas' competition. I won it, and got £5 and a beautiful sash that the judge draped around my waist.

I came home more excited than I'd ever been before. My mother and father were in bed. I sneaked in, and my father heard me. 'Is that you, Sheila?'

'Yes, it's me, and look what I have got.'

He started to lecture me and began shouting, but when I handed him the envelope with the £5 in it, he changed his tune. 'The money is for you, Dad,' I said as I gave it to him, and he was well pleased. £5 was a lot of money away back then in the early 50s.

One thing hurt me about winning the Miss Christmas competition. It was never put in the local newspaper as any other big event always was. I wonder why.

I worked in the hotel happily, and still did some raspberry work on my days off (which I never got paid for, because it was for the family).

Early the next year, I had a crush on one of the Wallace Arnold bus drivers. He was much older than me, and knocked me back because he was a married man.

In these days no girl, especially of the traveller community, had sex with any of their boyfriends, and the boys respected that. It was only a cuddle and a kiss and going for walks.

One weekend we went up to Huntly, visiting my father's cousins. We had heard they were in bow tents up there, about a mile out of Huntly, so we packed our gate-leg tent and took to the road. We arrived in the late afternoon. They were so pleased to see us. The men put up our gate-leg tent with my father, we built a big fire at the door of the tent, and my mother put the kettle on for tea. All the children were playing about happily as if they hadn't a care in the world. Looking back now and comparing them to kids these days, I can safely say I have never seen the same contentment on their faces as we had then.

My mother, my sister Cathie and me went to the shop for some groceries. It was an old-fashioned shop that sold everything from the needle eye to the anchor, as we would say then. When we went in there was an old woman talking, or in fact arguing, with the woman behind the counter. The old woman had a very withered face, she was bent over, and she had an old raggedy shawl round her shoulders. She was swearing like a trooper at the shopkeeper. As far as we could tell she was wanting more chukky (stuff on tick), and the shopkeeper wouldn't give her any.

'I want my drink!' she was shouting at the woman. 'If I don't get it, you will suffer, my lady.'

In through the door came a policeman. 'Well, Moira, what are you causing trouble for now?'

'It's this stupid woman, Wull, she won't give me my whisky.'

'Now, now, be off with you and don't cause any more bother,' said the policeman.

'You are as bad as that filthy hoor of a shopkeeper,' said the old woman.

The policeman went to take her arm and lead her out of the shop.

Just then she fell to the ground. The policeman knelt down beside her and took her pulse. Then he lifted his head and said to the shopkeeper, 'She's dead.'

'Thank God,' said the woman behind the counter, 'she won't torment us any more.'

I thought to myself, what a hard thing to say about a poor old woman. We were completely ignored by the shopkeeper and the police, as if we weren't there. We got our groceries eventually and headed out of the shop, leaving the woman and the policeman joking and laughing about the poor old creature's death.

9

I Become a Soldier

❧

I think my most mixed-up year was when I was 17. I passed my driving test, and then had to join the army, the Women's Royal Army Corps. A family crisis led to me being forced to join up. I applied with a friend, but she didn't pass the medical and I did, so off I went down to Guildford in Surrey to start my army career.

I had never been away from the bosom of my family before, and you can imagine the fear I was feeling, on a train by myself, heading for England. I arrived at the station in Guildford about seven at night, and was met by a sergeant. There were ten of us being picked up. I cannot think of a time in my life that I had as much fear in me as at that moment coming into the station.

We were taken to our barracks and shouted at a lot. We could make our own tea but got nothing to eat when we arrived. None of us slept much that night, with our bellies rumbling with hunger. Next morning we were woken up at six by a shouting NCO (non-commissioned officer).

I must tell you about our breakfast that morning. We got porridge with no salt in it (I was used to eating it with salt), and the milk was watered-down condensed milk. Yuck! I can taste it till this day.

After breakfast we went to meet the Captain, to sign up for our wages and receive our army number. Mine was Pte Stewart, 19198443. We were not to be allowed off camp for two weeks. Our duties were to prepare for our passing-out parade, a lot of marching and square-bashing. When we were practising for the parade, I was chosen one morning to be the left marker. It meant the squad had to follow me, and I had to keep them in a straight line. It was quite an honour for me. I also got great credit for my kit being perfectly ironed. My brother gave me two tips on how to make a perfect crease – firstly, don't use a damp cloth to iron, use damp brown paper; and secondly, run soap down the inside of the seam, and when it is dry it will hold the crease together.

After the two weeks were up we were allowed to go into town. One of the girls came to me and said, 'Sheila, I have a date with my boyfriend tonight. He is in the men's camp in Aldershot, and he wants me to bring a friend as a blind date for his pal.' I was shocked at being asked, but happy at the same time. Anything to get out of camp for the night.

We got the bus into Guildford, which was only a couple of miles away, and were met by the two soldiers. I was so embarrassed and so was my blind date. His name was Keith Swift. He was tall, moderately good-looking, and he was a gentleman.

I went with Keith for a few weeks, and they were very happy weeks, just getting to know each other. He was from a better-class family than me, with plenty of money and an estate. Or rather, his father owned the estate.

Two days before the passing-out parade, the major sent for me. I went to his office, and he told me that my father had bought me out of the army as the family problem had been solved. My father had paid £20 to get me out. I had to leave on the day of the passing-out parade. I was shattered, because I wanted to pass out after all that work.

The next night I met Keith and had to tell him I was going home. He was devastated at the news, but I told him that in our family we didn't say no to my father. We exchanged addresses. The next day I left the army, and that was the end of my army career.

When I got home I received a letter a day from Keith. He said he wanted to come up to my home town Blairgowrie to visit me. I panicked at this idea. No, I thought, he can't come up. So I had to write to him and tell him I was a traveller.

After that, his pal phoned me and said Keith wanted all his letters back and never wanted to hear from me again. I sent all the letters back, and said I was sorry I hadn't told him sooner. Two weeks later I got a letter from his pal saying Keith was distraught.

When I came home I got my job back in the hotel again. I was glad to be back home, really. No more non-travellers for me, I had learned my lesson. Well, that's what I thought, anyway. I grew up during the time I was in the army, and it was probably all for the better.

I had really missed going camping and staying with travellers. On my first weekend back we went down to Dumfries, camping. We put up our tent in a quarry just outside the town. When our camp was up, a tall man approached us and said he was a traveller. His name was Joe Morrison. He stayed in a house nearby with his mother and father and two sisters, and asked us if we would come down to see them that night. He gave us the address and was waiting at his door when we arrived. The whole family were jewels of people. They were dying to have a talk with other travellers and have a ceilidh round their fire. So we fixed up the ceilidh for the next night. They were so excited. My father was pleased he had brought his pipes with him, and we knew it would be a real good night.

The following evening my father, mother, sister Rena and myself arrived at the house. Joe was waiting at the door for us again, and welcomed us in. There was a spread on the table fit for a gourmet. It was all travellers' food: ham shanks, a pot of broth, ham ribs, oxtail (my father was the only one who ate the oxtail) and a clootie (cloth) dumpling.

We sat and ate our fill. We were grunting with the pain in our bellies from overeating. Then we sat for about an hour before the singing and stories started. Just before it, a knock came to the door and a woman and a midget man came in. I was gasping and so was Rena – we had never seen such a small man in our lives. They were introduced to us and they were man and wife. Joe's mother, Aggie, made tea for everyone, and fed the newly arrived couple. Then the ceilidh began.

My father started with the bagpipes. His first tune was 'Leaving Lismore', then he played 'The Maid Behind the Bar' and 'The Devil in the Kitchen'.

After the pipe tunes, Joe turned to the wee man and said, 'Willie, it's your turn now.' Rena and I looked at each other, not knowing what to expect. Well, Willie opened his mouth and we were all dumbstruck. He sang opera. I thought to myself, how can such a wee man have a voice like that, but we got a bigger surprise when his wife joined him in the song. She was a soprano. Opera is not my type of music, but it sounded great.

Then Aggie sang a song about travellers pulling flax and gathering potatoes. It was a homemade wee song. She had a good voice, but the song wasn't up to much.

Joe did some canterach, traditional mouth music, a slow air he had composed himself. He called it 'Joe's Walk', which I thought a peculiar name, but it was a nice tune.

My mother, instead of singing, recited a poem she had made up.

It's a Hard Life Being a Traveller

> It happened at the berryfields,
> When the travellers came to Blair,
> They pitched their tents on the berryfields,
> Without a worry or care.
>
> But they hadn't been long settled there,
> When some heed yins came fae Perth,
> And told them they must go at once,
> And get off the face of the earth.
>
> These folk of course were worried,
> For of law they had no sense,
> They only came to the berryfields,
> To earn a few honest pence.

But it was very hard to keep them there,
When the policemen said to go,
So they just packed up, and took the road,
To where? I do not know.

It's a hard life being a traveller,
I have proved it to be true,
I have tried in every possible way,
To live with times that's new.

But we're always hit below the belt,
No matter what we do,
But when it comes to our judgement day,
We'll be just the same as you.

I looked up at Aggie and the tears were running down her cheeks. She got up and hugged my mother, and said, 'Belle, that was great. Could you write it out for me, and Joe will read it to me now and again?' She wasn't able to read herself.

10
Courting and Singing

One day a friend of mine who stayed round the corner knocked on my door. 'Sheila,' she said, 'will you come to the dance with me tonight, it's in the Angus Hotel this week. Oh, I am so excited. An old boyfriend of mine is home on leave from the army, and he is going to the dance. You know I can't go on my own.'

I looked at her and said, 'But you are living with somebody, and you have a baby to him.'

'Yes, I know,' she replied, 'but I have always fancied him. Please, Sheila, come with me.'

I agreed, and we went to the dance in the Angus Hotel. It was a Saturday night, the main night for dancing. I went into the toilet to hang my coat up. When I came out she was standing near the door waiting. 'He is not here yet, but it's early still.'

An hour afterwards she came over to me and said, 'He has just came in with his pals.'

'What is his name?' I asked.

'Ian MacGregor,' she answered.

'Point him out to me,' I said. He was dressed in his army uniform.

Just then, a traveller who kept wanting to take me out asked me for a dance.

The dance carried on, and Ian MacGregor never spoke to my friend or danced with her once. She was fuming with rage. To pacify I told her he would probably ask her to dance the last dance, and then would want to know if he could take her home. She calmed down then.

71

At the second last dance, the traveller boy asked if he could take me home.

'No,' I said.

'Oh well, I will wait for you outside at the door.'

My friend and I were waiting for the last waltz to start, and she grabbed me by the arm. 'He is coming over!' she said. But instead of asking her for the last dance, he asked me.

I was mortified. Asking for the last dance meant he would want to take me home. I looked over at my friend standing there and she was fizzing.

As we were dancing he asked to take me home. I was so shocked I blurted out that my friend was expecting him to ask her home.

'I'm not taking her home, she has a man and a kid,' he said.

'Well, my friend is taking me home, and he asked before you did,' was my answer.

He smiled and said, 'See you outside.'

I went for my coat. My friend told me Ian hadn't asked to take her home. I couldn't tell her he had asked me. We put our coats on and came out of the hotel. My traveller friend smiled at me. Ian was standing next to him, and when I came out, he stepped forward, took me by the arm and said, 'Run!' We ran down the road until we were out of sight of the others.

I asked him again why he had done this. He simply said, 'I wanted to take you home.'

Now I was really worried. The thought that a non-traveller from my town wanted to go out with me was a miracle. I knew all his family; he had seven sisters and six brothers. If they knew he was seeing a traveller, all hell would break loose.

I didn't say anything about this that night. He took me home, we had a wee snog, and he asked me out to the pictures the next Wednesday. I said yes, I would go with him.

The next day I told my mother I had a date on Wednesday. 'Oh, no,' she said, 'we are getting a visit from someone from the School of Scottish Studies.' It was our first visit from Hamish Henderson.

Hamish's visit meant I couldn't go to my date on the Wednesday, but my sister Cathie and her man were going to the pictures that night, and I asked them to tell Ian, if he was standing waiting for me, that I couldn't come. But when they came home they said they had forgotten to do it. I was so disappointed.

That first visit from Hamish was one of many through the years. He came that Wednesday night and the first thing I sang to him was 'She Moved through the Fair'. My mother got the song in Ireland, and it went like this:

> My young love said to me, 'My mother won't mind,
> And my father won't slight you for your lack of kind,'
> Then she stepped away from me, and this she did say,
> 'It will not be long, love, till our wedding day.'
>
> Then she stepped away from me, and she moved
> through the fair,
> And fondly I watched her move here and move there,
> And as she went homeward with one star awake,
> Like the swan in the evening moved over the lake.
>
> Last night she came to me, my dead love came in,
> So softly she came that her feet made no din,
> As she laid her hand on me, twas this she did say,
> 'It will not be long, love, till our wedding day.'

That was the start of the collectors coming to our house. Every other day we had microphones stuck in our faces.

One story my mother told to him that Hamish liked was the 'Beech Hedge Wager'.

This old tramp man went into a pub in Perth one night. I don't know how long ago it was, but it was a long, long time ago. Well, he was down and out, he hadn't even enough money for a half pint of beer, and he was dying for a drink.

There were a few toffs in the pub that night. They were standing at the end of the bar drinking their pints, and the poor tramp man was licking his lips looking at them.

They were discussing the seven wonders of the world, and about all the wonderful things they had seen. One of them started showing off about a horse he had, and how it couldn't be beaten at jumping. He said there wasn't a hedge or a dyke or a fence his horse couldn't jump.

Now the tramp man was listening to their conversation. So he went up to the toffs and said, 'Excuse me, sir, I just overheard what you said, that you have a grand horse, and he is a great jumper.'

'Yes, my man, I have that.' They didn't want to entertain the old tramp man in conversation at all, however they couldn't turn him away.

'I am a poor tramp man,' said the tramp, 'but I bet you one hundred pounds I can take you to a hedge that your horse can't jump. The toffs were interested to hear this, a poor old tramp man betting a hundred pounds. So they agreed to take the bet.

The tramp man took them to the Meikleour Beech Hedge outside Perth, which is over 120 feet high. The tramp won his bet, and got the hundred pounds.

Hamish collected a lot of material that night from our family. We knew nothing about this tall academic at that time, and we kept things short, not knowing what he was really after. Hamish didn't rush us either, he was cautious too. He let us decide what to record.

The next night the recording session got heavier. We sang more ballads to him, like 'The Twa Brothers'.

> Two pretty boys were going tae the school,
> And one evening coming home,
> Said William to John, 'Can you throw a stone,
> Or can you play at a ball,
> Or can you play at a ball?'

Said William to John, 'I cannot throw a stone,
Nor little can I play at a ball,
But if you come down to yon merry green woods,
I'll try you a wrestling fall,
I'll try you a wrestling fall.'

So they cam' doon tae yon merry green woods,
Beneath the spreading moon
And the little penknife slipped out of William's pocket,
And gave John his deadly wound,
And gave John his deadly wound.

'You take off your white Holland shirt,
And tear it from gore to gore:
And you will bind my deadly wounds,
And they will bleed no more,
And they will bleed no more.'

So he took off his white Holland shirt,
And tore it from gore to gore,
And he did bind his deadly wounds,
But they bled ten times more,
But they bled ten times more.

'What will I tell to your sister dear,
This night when I go home?'
'You can tell her I'm away to a London school,
And a good scholar I'll come home,
And a good scholar I'll come home.'

'And what will I tell to your sweetheart dear,
This night when I go home?'
'You can tell her I'm dead and in grave laid,
And the grass is growing green,
And the grass is growing green.'

'And what will I tell to your father dear,
This night when I go home?'
'You can tell him I'm dead and in grave laid,
And the grass is growing green,
And the grass is growing green.'

'And what will I tell to your stepmother dear,
This night when I go home?'
'You can tell her I'm dead and in grave laid,
For she prayed I might never come home,
For she prayed I might never come home.'

A few years later Hamish told us that this was the oldest version of 'The Twa Brothers' he had ever collected, and that it dated back to the twelfth century.

11

Engagement

🍃

After our recording sessions, Hamish left to go back to Edinburgh to unload his tapes and get more blank ones.

The following Saturday I went to the dance again, which that week was in the town hall. I got there about eight-thirty and danced a few dances. At nine o'clock Ian came in. I was so ashamed because I had stood him up on our date. He came over and I explained to him what had happened, and how Cathie had forgotten to tell him. Right there and then he asked to take me home that night, at the end of the dance, and I said yes.

As you can imagine, my friend with her own man and baby never spoke to me again for many years, though she did try to split us up a year later. Ian and I started going out steady after that, but he wasn't happy when I couldn't see him on the days when Hamish came to tape us. Every time there was an argument.

We seemed to argue a lot because of his jealousy. He was the most jealous man I had ever met. Even if I wasn't there and a man paid me a compliment, he would punch him in the face. 'Keep your hands off,' he would say.

We had some good times together, but I wondered why he never took me to meet his family. Instead he was in our house all the time. One day I asked him why, and was it because I was a traveller.

'Yes,' he replied, 'they are all snobs. I like the way your family live, they are real people. I love the travellers' outlook on life. So forget about my family, because they will never come round.' So that's what I did. When I think about it now, he must have gone through hell, but me being young and used to being treated this way all my life, I paid no attention to his side of things.

Every time I went singing with the family there was an argument. I couldn't say no to my father and mother, and he didn't understand this.

I remember we went to Edinburgh to do our first concert, in an old church. There was my mother, father, Jeannie Robertson, old Jimmy MacBeath, Davie Stewart (my father's cousin, the Auld Galoot as we called him), a folk group and a few more artists, myself and Cathie. We all went up individually to the pulpit to do our turn, and the acoustics were wonderful.

After the concert we were all invited back to Hamish's flat for a cup of tea. We all piled in, and Hamish was three sheets to the wind as usual. We all thought we were going to be paid, and that is why we went back to the flat. One of the members of the folk group asked Hamish for their money, because they needed petrol for their van to get back to Glasgow.

'Oh, I am sorry!' said Hamish, 'I have run out of cheques.'

We all looked at each other in shock. The members of the folk group had a word together, and then said to Hamish, 'We don't need cheques.' One of the musicians handed him sheets of toilet paper from one of the old-fashioned slippery rolls.

'The banks will accept these.'

'No, they won't,' said Hamish.

'I guarantee they will,' said the man, 'because I am a lawyer when I am not playing with the group, and I know it for a fact.'

Well, I wish I had had a camera that night; Hamish's face was a picture. That was the only time Hamish gave us anything for performing for him, and it was on bum paper. The bank took the the sheets as valid cheques. We got £5 each – £20 altogether for the Stewarts of Blair. In those days that was worth something.

As a family we had our own berryfields for many years before I was married. My brother Andy had a farm called the Cleaves. I remember one day when my uncle Donald came to see us there during the berry-picking and he stayed for a few hours to help out. He was weighing the berries, and I was paying out the money to all the berry-pickers.

Then we saw a gang of young men coming along the road. It was a lovely day, so warm that the sun was melting the tar on the road, and the youths were jumping up and down, bursting the bubbles with their bare feet. They were squealing like mad with the heat of the tar, but giggling at the same time. There were about ten young men altogether, all wearing leather jackets decked with chains. We knew this was a gang from Glasgow who were staying at Essendy, a couple of miles away.

'Sheila, be careful,' my uncle Donald whispered, 'they might be after the money.'

I was nervous, I must admit, especially as I had just got the money box rimming full of cash to pay the berry-pickers. In my nervousness, when they approached and said hello, my hand hit the box and the money scattered all over the ground. I was terrified then, because immediately they all made a dive for the money. But to our surprise, they lifted every penny for me and put it back in the box. We couldn't believe it. 'Sorry if we feared you, Miss, but I think it is all back in now,' said one, in a heavy Glaswegian accent.

They were the nicest boys we met that year. After they had gone, my uncle Donald said to me, 'Sheila, you should never judge a book by its cover.' I smiled at him and nodded.

When my brother Andy came down from the farm he asked us if everything was alright. Me and my uncle Donald burst out laughing, and uncle Donald said, 'Couldn't be better.' We never did tell anyone else what happened that day; it was our secret.

One Saturday around that time, Ian and I went to the dance in the town hall again. We were going to meet at the dance itself, because Ian wanted to go to the pub first. In those days the pubs closed at nine-thirty. There was a friend of mine at the dance that night who I hadn't seen for a long time. (In later life he went on to become a famous newscaster.) He came up and asked me for a dance, a modern waltz, and I went with him. He asked if I would partner him for the next foxtrot, and I said yes. By the time it came to the foxtrot, Ian had come in and was standing beside me as my friend came up and nodded for me to dance. Then Ian stepped in. He grabbed my old friend by the collar and said, 'Here, pal, what are you on about?'

'Sheila said I could have this foxtrot.'

'Oh, she did, did she?'

The next thing I knew, they were fighting all over the hall. Everybody at the dance stopped and watched, and I ran screaming into the toilet, with my cousin following me. I hated fighting. The fight continued for twenty minutes, then a few of the boys stopped it. Somebody came into the toilet and told me it was all over, and that Ian was waiting for me outside.

I was fuming. I looked at him with his face all covered in blood, and I told him there and then that we were finished. He managed to persuade me to let him see me home. We never spoke a word all the way.

My mother was standing at the door when we arrived, and when she saw his face, she went mad and took him in to wash his face. 'Sheila,' she said, 'The poor laddie, have you no sympathy for him?'

'No, I haven't. I never want to see him again.'

My father came on the scene then, wondering what was going on. When he saw Ian's face, he said, 'Who done that to you, laddie?'

Then I chimed in, 'He fought with a laddie that just asked me to dance, and he went berserk.'

'That shows you how much he thinks about you,' said my father.

I ran to my room where Rena was already asleep. Fuming with rage, I crawled into bed and soon fell asleep.

The next morning when I got up and went into the kitchen, Ian was having toast and tea with my mother and father. He had a black eye and a jeely nose (as Oor Wullie would say). By this time I had calmed down a bit. I began to feel sorry for him then, and we made up. I told him straight, we weren't married and he had no business doing what he had done. He apologised, though not very convincingly.

The next week my father asked the family if we wanted to go pearl-fishing on the Sunday, and we said yes. He also asked Ian, and he wanted to go too. Ian was so excited about it, because he had never been pearl-fishing before. He had never even heard there was such a thing.

We packed up that Sunday and a crowd of us headed for the Dochart. We took sandwiches with us, and chitties (a stand to hang the kettle over the fire) for our tea. I was excited because I had Ian with me, and I felt that the family were accepting him.

It was an enjoyable day, except for one thing – Ian was the only one who got a pearl! It was about ten grains, round and pink, a cracker. That didn't sit well with my uncles. His first time and he got a pearl. They spoke about it for weeks, jealous because of his success. It meant he wasn't very popular with them, but no matter what boyfriend I had come with, they wouldn't have considered he was good enough for me anyway.

I had fallen out with Ian during the week that followed, but decided to go to the dance with my cousin anyway. Ian didn't turn up, and I was disappointed.

When I came out of the town hall at the end of the dance, he was standing across the road hiding in a doorway. I went over to him and asked him what he was doing there, and he said he was watching to see if I was going to go home with somebody else. We made it up as usual. It was a peculiar kind of love we had, but very deep. We couldn't agree, yet couldn't stay away from each other.

This sort of thing went on for the next two years. We squabbled all the time because of his jealousy. Then, at Christmas 1955, Ian, my cousin Norman and myself went to a dance in Alyth, five miles away.

We were dancing, Ian and I, when he looked into my eyes and said, 'Will you marry me?' I laughed and said 'No'. He walked off the floor and went out of the door with Norman in tow.

Norman came back in, very angry with me. 'Ian is devastated, Sheila, why did you say no?'

'I thought he was joking. Go back with this message for him, tell him to ask me again outside.'

Norman returned and told me Ian was waiting for me outside. Smiling to myself, and very excited, I headed for the door.

As I came down the steps, he was leaning with his back against the wall, with head bent. I walked up to him, lifted his chin up and kissed him on the lips, whispering all the time, 'Yes, yes, yes!'

We were both gloriously happy that night. He told me I would get the engagement ring in a couple of days. I didn't know then that when he asked me to marry him I was two months pregnant. When I found out, I was glad he had asked me before either of us knew about the baby.

12

Marriage and a Baby

❧

On 28 January 1956, Ian and I were married in the registry office in Rattray. There were only five of us there. Our best man was Bruce, a friend of Ian's, and my bridesmaid was Margaret, daughter of friends of ours, Frank and Ruby, from Banff. Ian didn't have the seven shillings and sixpence that had to be paid for the license after the ceremony. So my father paid for the license.

Only Ian's mother and one of his sisters came to the small reception we held in the living room of my parents' house, where my mother had laid on a spread.

For our honeymoon we hired a caravan for a week and put it at the end of a field called the 'Witch's Knowe' belonging to my brother John. It was a wee whoopee trailer, as we called it in these days, only twelve feet long. A horrible wee thing it was. It had one gas ring, and was falling apart.

As it was January, it was bitterly cold. We had a small paraffin heater, but the fumes it gave off were too bad for us to leave it on, so we turned the gas ring on for heat. It was warm when you stood up, but cold when you sat down.

After our first night in the wee caravan we needed paraffin for the heater. Ian had cleaned it in the morning so that it would not give off any fumes. We headed over the back road to my parents' house, and on the way went into the shop to buy a gallon of fuel. We went up to my parents' house to get warm for a while, but didn't tell them that.

When we left we had to pass the George Hotel, and Ian dropped the bombshell. 'Sheila, you go up to the trailer with the paraffin, I am going into the pub for a drink. I will be home later.'

I was mortified that he could leave me on the second day of our honeymoon. I walked up the road, slipping on the ice all the way.

When I got to the caravan, Ian's brother was there paying a visit to see how we were getting on. Then I discovered that Ian had the key of the caravan in his pocket, so I couldn't get in. I was shivering with cold reaching right through to my bones.

Ian's brother crawled through the wee window of the caravan and opened the door for me. He filled up the heater with paraffin and lit it. I put the kettle on and made him a cup of tea, and as we were drinking it, Ian walked through the door.

'What's going on here,' he said, looking at his brother angrily. 'What are you doing here, are you after my wife?'

I was very embarrassed, after the help his brother had given me.

'Why did you leave your wife to go to a pub on your second day of marriage, you fool?' shouted his brother. Ian made a dive at him and they fell out of the door of the caravan, struggling with each other. His brother got up and shouted something at Ian which I couldn't hear, and went home.

'What did you give him a cup of tea for, we only got married yesterday, it is too soon for visitors. Did he try it on with you?'

I was horrified at his suggestion. 'No, he did not!'

I explained to Ian about him having the caravan key in his pocket, and his brother crawling through the window to let me in. All he said was, 'Don't let anyone in if I am not here.'

That was the end of the conversation. It shook me to the core. Ian was even jealous of his own brother. That didn't say much for me either. I wasn't that type of person. Could he not see that I was a one-man woman? Ian just said, 'No woman can be trusted, as far as I am concerned.'

After the week was up and they came and collected the caravan, my uncle Donald gave us a single-end in Yeaman Street, Rattray. We were charged no rent for it. He furnished it for us as well. It was a comfortable wee room and we were happy there.

Me at the age of 4, 'The Marmalade Can'.

My Uncle Donald, who taught me the ballads when I was a young girl.

Traditional travellers in their camp.

My father, Alex Stewart, with his bagpipes.

Me at the age of 10.

My Uncle Hendry playing the pipes.

Me winning the Miss Christmas competition in Blairgowrie when I was 17.

My mother and me.

Hamish Henderson, the first time he came to see us.

Ian and me on our wedding day.

Me in Hatfield in the 1960s.

With Ian and the family in England.

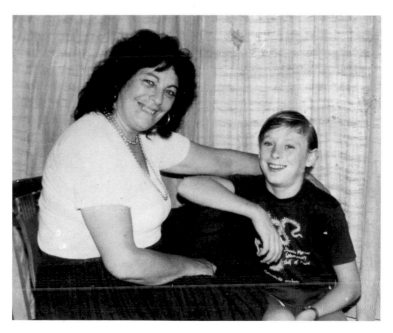

Me with Roy.

The Stewarts o' Blair at Lake Como, Italy: Cathie, me, son Ian and my mother.

My mother with me on her 90th birthday.

Ian had a wood-cutting job to go to on the Monday. I cried because I didn't want him to go and leave me, so he didn't go, and lost his job.

My uncle Donald came to me a few weeks later and said he had folk who wanted to rent the house, so we had to get out. We moved in with my mother and father.

At the beginning of May I took ill and collapsed. My mother sent for the doctor who examined me. I had a terrible pain in my left side and I was screaming with it. The doctor said it was the baby pressing on my side, that it would get better in a few days, and gave me painkillers.

About a week later the pain got worse, and my mother sent for the doctor again. It was a different lady doctor this time, and she sent for an ambulance to take me to the Friarton hospital in Perth, a hospital for tuberculosis. The head surgeon examined me. What he discovered was that it was neglected pleurisy, and they had to aspirate (draw the fluid off) my left lung. I was critically ill and I was drowning in my own fluid. Yet if I had been put into hospital a week earlier I would have been fine.

An hour after being taken to the Friarton I was in the operating room. I wasn't allowed to lie on a trolley; I had to sit facing the back of the chair with my hands draped over it. I was in agony.

Then they took a big hollow needle, connected to a pump. They put it into me, pierced my left lung and started to pump the fluid off my lung. They got two and a half pints off the first time. I fainted with the pain, and was taken to my bed heavily sedated.

Two days later I woke up, and Ian and my mother were standing at my bedside. I was so weak I couldn't speak. The doctor was also there telling them what had happened to me. The only thing I can remember hearing was his words, 'Touch and go.'

The pleurisy had gone into tuberculosis. I was worried about the baby and tried to speak, moving the bed covers. Ian knew what I was meaning and stopped me. 'Sheila, the baby is fine,' he said. Then they were asked to leave. He kissed me and so did my mother.

I don't remember much about the first week I was in hospital, except that they aspirated me twice more. They got a pint of fluid the second time and a bit less than a pint the third time.

During the second week the doctor in charge came to speak to me. Ian and my father were with him. 'You will not be allowed out of bed for at least seven months. I think the tablets will dry your lungs up now, but you will have to stay flat on your back, with one pillow, for all that time.'

Ian was holding my hand, and I just burst into tears. 'What about my baby?' I said.

'Oh, the baby is fine,' said the doctor. 'When it is due we will transfer you to Perth maternity ward. You will have the baby, but you won't be able to see it or touch it till you are discharged from this hospital.'

I was devastated. I was facing seven months' lying on my back, giving birth to my baby and not being able to see it or hold it. I was in a state of complete shock. My father kept telling me, 'Sheila, me and your mother will take the baby, and Ian will be there. We will look after it till you come home.' That didn't settle me and I cried all the more. The nurse asked them to leave, and I was heavily sedated again. I was asleep for three days that time.

On the next Sunday my uncle Hendry came in to see me. He had walked all the way out of town to the hospital on his own. He was 84. When he came in he was sweating like a pig, it was running down his face. The nurse came and offered him a drink, and a towel to wipe himself down.

'Now, Marmalade Can,' (that was his nickname for me), 'I have come to learn you a song.' Even when I was ill, my family wanted me to learn their songs.

'It is called "The Bonny Green Tree". I think it will be the last one I can learn you, 'cause I am getting auld now.' He took out his hankie and wiped his nose.

I grabbed him by the hand, saying, 'No, no!'

Then he started to sing. The nurse came to the bed and jotted down the words for me, so I only had to learn the tune.

Bonny Green Tree.

One fine summer's morning, as I was a-walking,
One fine summer's morning, as it happened to be,
I espied a young damsel, she appeared like an angel,
She was under the shade of a bonny green tree.

I stepped up to her, just for to view her,
And I said 'My pretty fair maid, your looks entice me,
I will make you a lady of high rich and honour,
If you grant me the shade of your bonny green tree.'

'Ah, but I'm not a lady of high rich and honour,
I am only a poor girl as it happened to be,
And your friends and relations they will pass you like
                                                    a stranger,
And then they will leave you, as my love left me.'

And then she sat down and I sat down beside her,
And under the bushes she vowed to wed me,
But when I approached her I found her a virgin,
'Tomorrow we'll get married, but a bride you'll never be.'

So, come all you fair maids, now take a warning,
Never heed the false words that a young man might say,
For he'll promise to wed you, and then he will leave you,
Then he will leave you, as my love left me.

By the time uncle Hendry was finished, tears were pouring down my cheeks, and he had to use his hankie again many times before the end.

'The saddest thing for me,' he said, 'is that I won't hear you sing it.' He bent down to me, but the nurse had to raise the bed so I could kiss him.

There wasn't a dry eye in that large ward. They made him

a cup of tea, and wouldn't let him walk home. They paid for a taxi for him, for entertaining all the other patients. He died soon after that.

I was admitted to hospital on 8 May, and I took ill to have my baby on 7 August. He was born on 8 August.

Ian came in to visit me not long after our son was born. When he asked the nurse if he could see our child, she said, 'No, you can't see your baby.'

Ian looked at her in dismay. 'Why not?' he asked.

'I will get the doctor to speak to you.'

When the doctor came in he told us that Ian couldn't see our son because I had TB, and it could spread from us to the baby. Ian was not a happy man and was angry the whole visit, not with me but with the hospital.

A week later I was taken back to the Friarton, and the baby went home to Ian. He decided to call him Ian after himself.

I returned to my old ward, and the other patients cheered when I was brought back to my bed. We had a party for my coming back. But I was so upset about not seeing the baby, I had to be sedated all over again.

Next day Ian and my father came in to see me, and told me that the baby had been named Ian. I was so pleased to see them. At that point I felt I was outside my family for the first time in my life. But as usual my father cheered me up with his funny remarks about the baby.

The patient in the bed opposite me was very, very, ill. After they had gone, she looked over at me and said, 'Sheila, you know how ill I am. Well, I promise to stay alive till you go home, no matter how long that will take.' I was so pleased that she wasn't going to give in to her illness, and was willing to fight for my sake.

That night she took a bad turn and the doctor was called. I didn't sleep that night, listening to them running back and forward. In the morning she was sitting up eating her breakfast. 'You'll no' get rid of me that easily, Sheila. Remember my promise.'

13
Married Life

❧

When the baby was three months old, the doctor said my mother and Ian could bring him to the hospital, if they stayed outside and held him up to the window so that I could see him. The nurses propped me up in my bed and raised the bed so that I could look out of the window. Ian held him up to the window, and he was dressed like a wee elf.

That was the first and only time I saw him until I was allowed out of the hospital. I can still see him till this day in my mind's eye, dressed like a wee elf.

When the time was right and I could get out of bed, I had to learn to walk all over again. When I put my feet on the floor it was like someone was pushing needles into the soles of them. I fell back into the bed with my face all distorted with pain.

'Come on, now,' said the nurse, 'that pain will go away soon. Try again, and hold on to me.'

It was three hours that day before I could try walking again, but very slowly.

The first time I walked up the ward was wonderful for the rest of the patients: they clapped and cheered, and my friend cried her eyes out. I went over and cuddled and kissed her. 'Oh, Sheila, you shouldn't have kissed me – I have TB.'

I looked at her and laughed and said, 'So do I.' We laughed and laughed, and that cheered us up no end.

Ian got a great shock when he came in a few days later. I was sitting up on a chair, and told him I could walk round the grounds with him. The look on his face was a picture.

Slowly we walked round the grounds, where we found a garden summerhouse for patients to sit in. I won't tell you all that happened in that summerhouse. That was between Ian and me. I was allowed to stay up till I got tired, then they put me to bed.

I went into hospital, as I said, on the 8th of May, had my wee boy on the 8th of August and was discharged on the 8th of December. Leaving the rest of my friends on the ward was heartbreaking. After all, they were my family for seven months. My friend in the bed opposite was still alive when I left. She kept her promise.

My parents, with Ian and baby Ian, came to collect me to take me home. That was one of the happiest days of my life. On the way home, I was told that my uncle Hendry had died. I learned his song as he taught me. I sing it often, but only to him as I see him in my mind's eye, and I am sure he hears me singing.

We called the baby Totie (small) Ian and his father Big Ian. I felt sorry for Big Ian at that time, he wasn't allowed to be a proper father to Totie. My mother and father took him over. I was hardly allowed to hold him for long either.

We longed for a house of our own. Ian had put our name down with the council for a house. Things got pretty bad, and about a month later Ian and I started to argue again about who should be looking after the baby. I couldn't go against my parents' wishes, it just wasn't done. Ian walked out and said he was not coming back. I was devastated. I should have stuck up for him that day.

He went to Glasgow to go to work on the docks. I became ill and took to my bed.

A day later my bedroom door opened and in he came. He was bedraggled and looked so sad. I thought it was because of us being apart, but it was much worse. He had witnessed one of his work mates getting his head chopped off by a huge fat heavy chain. His friend had been standing about ten feet away from Ian. His body started to run about with the nerves, and Ian and another mate had to chase it and jump on it to stop it.

Ian burst into tears while he was telling me the story. It plagued him for weeks. He relived the scene every night in his sleep and had nightmares about it. He never went back to Glasgow to work, but stayed with me.

We lodged with my parents for another few months, then we got a house of our own from the council. It was a relief to have our own home at last, so that Ian could be a real father to Totie.

Ian at that time started a band and took bookings for gigs. I never saw any money from what he was earning as a musician, I think he drank it all.

One day my father's sister, Bella, came to see me in a panic. I was on my own. My mother was looking after my son, and Ian wasn't in. 'Oh, Sheila,' she said, 'there is a woman in my house from the berryfields, and she is choking. You must come, I don't know what to do with her.'

I put my coat on and followed auntie Bella to her house. It was only just down the road in the next scheme.

My cousin William was in the house, holding the woman's hand and trying to comfort her. She was crying and choking. I looked down her throat but couldn't see anything. Then I remembered a story my grandfather had told me about a similar case that had happened in Ireland many years ago. There was a possible cure and something told me to try it. What else could I do? If I didn't try it she would choke to death.

I turned to my auntie Bella and asked her if she had a bit of raw beef or steak.

'Beef, yes, but no steak. Steak's too expensive for me,' she said, and gave a bit of a giggle. 'What are you going to do, Sheila?'

'Don't ask me just now, Auntie. If it is going to work, we have no time to lose,' I said. 'Get a scarf and blindfold her.'

Auntie Bella looked at me, puzzled, but she obeyed and brought the scarf.

Now I said to my cousin, 'William, blindfold her.'

'Why?' he asked.

'Never mind why, just do it,' I said.

'Auntie, now listen to me carefully. Hold her mouth as wide open as you can, and don't let it close.'

As auntie Bella held her mouth open, I took the bit of beef and held it near her tongue. After about five minutes she started to squirm, but we held her tight. After ten minutes a thing started to crawl out of her mouth towards the raw beef. It was a tapeworm, about three feet long. The smell of the beef had enticed it out.

The woman fell back, exhausted, as we all were. She coughed a bit, but had no more choking, and gave a sigh of relief. My cousin William and my auntie couldn't believe what they had just witnessed. I got a cup of tea, then after many cuddles of thank you from the woman, I went home.

A few days later, my mother and father came to our house and asked me and Totie to go with them on a run up to Aberfeldy. We always visited a farm-woman who lived there. Her man had died, and she and her son Peter ran the smallholding.

When we turned into the farmyard, memories came flooding back to me of when I was younger and I used to help the farmer milk the cows and make butter. As I thought of those days, I smiled to myself.

We got out of the car and went up to the front door. The lady of the house had not changed since I was a wee girl. We got a great welcome from her and were shown into the house. She put the kettle on.

She was looking very sad that day, and my father asked her what was wrong.

'Oh, Alex,' she said, 'it's about my Peter. You know Peter had one eye that squinted. He went to get it fixed in the hospital, and they operated on the wrong eye! Now he squints in both eyes. So he's back in hospital again, getting it fixed.'

My father, my mother and me couldn't help but laugh at what had happened to poor Peter. She saw the funny side of it as well when my father explained it to her.

We spent a couple of hours, and then we went home, taking with us eggs, butter, milk and tatties. On the way home, we couldn't stop thinking of poor Peter and laughing.

When I arrived home and told Ian about it, he thought it was funny too. He knew Peter very well, as while I was in hospital, he had got a job on the same Aberfeldy smallholding. He stayed in a tent on a field at the farm and used to hitch down to see me in hospital.

By this time I had fallen pregnant again. Things returned to normal. If Ian wasn't out practising with the band, he was doing gigs in the pub. It began to get on my nerves, especially as I was expecting again. He wasn't at home very much, so we argued a lot.

I always knew when Ian was coming home because our bedroom was near the road and he whistled all the way home. So I would prepare myself, either for an argument or I'd have a cup of tea ready for him. It would depend how drunk he was.

One night I sat up, waiting until he came home. When I heard his feet on the stairs, I threw a bag full of his clothes at him. After I threw it, I tripped on the top step and went flying down the stairs. Luckily he broke my fall, so I wasn't hurt and neither was the baby.

As usual, he was drunk. He crawled into bed and went to sleep. I went and sat in the living room and it was then that it struck me. Ian was not husband material. Although he adored his kids, he wasn't very family-oriented. But I loved him and I was his wife. I had made my bed, and I would have to lie in it.

14
The Stewarts o' Blair

When my second baby was due, I took ill at seven in the morning. Ian and I walked up to my parents' house, and the baby was born in one of the bedrooms at 9 a.m. It was another boy. I was very ill after the birth, but I soon recovered and things got back to normal. My second son was called Hamish. I wasn't allowed to choose any of my children's names, Ian chose them.

A month after Hamish was born, the Stewarts o' Blair got a booking in London. Cathie couldn't make it this time, so my father asked Ian if I could go. It was only for three days and we needed the money. He agreed very reluctantly, and Cathie said she would look after my two boys, if Ian helped her.

We set off for London the next day in my father's old banger. When we arrived, we found we were staying in a huge house that belonged to the people who were putting on the concert. We were very tired when we finally got there, especially my father, because he would not stop on the way until we had reached our destination.

When we pulled up in front of the big house, my father said, 'Belle, we've got a braw bed the night, thank goodness. I'm moudit wi' tiredness.'

We got a great welcome from the man and woman of the house, who were delighted that we had made it down. The woman said, 'Come in! Come in!' She had a meal ready for us. After the meal was when we got the shock. She and her husband were so excited about showing us where we were to sleep. To our surprise, they took us out the back door, and on the back lawn, they had built a bow tent. 'Here is a home from home for you. We wanted to make you feel at home,' said the woman.

We just looked at each other, and the expression on my father's face was quite a picture. But what could we do? They thought they were doing the right thing. It did not go down well with my parents, however.

The next night was the concert. It was being held in Islington, at one of the first folk clubs that really succeeded in London. From famous artists to MPs, anybody who was anybody came to the club that night. The concert was a great success. We performed ballads, songs and stories, and even featured my father with the pipes — many things the audience had never heard before.

When the concert was finished, people gathered around to congratulate us. The couple we were staying with invited some people they knew back for a party. My father and mother, along with the rest of the people, piled into two cars, but there was no room for me. There was an MP coming to the party as well, and he said I could get a lift in his car. He was a very famous politician in later years, but I won't tell you his name.

We drove through London to get to the house. When we were going along a particular street he told me to lock my door, as it was a very bad area. He said rough people lived there and we had to be careful. We were stopped at traffic lights when he suddenly grabbed my hand and put it between his legs. I said to him, 'It must be a really bad area, because you've got a cosh in your pocket!'

Then the cosh started to move, and I realised what it was. I pulled my hand away and jumped into the back of the car, screaming. When he heard the noise I made, I think he got a bigger fright than I had and couldn't apologise enough. I calmed down and told him I would never mention what he had done to anybody. By the time we got to the house, the two of us were behaving as if nothing had happened.

The party was in full swing. My mother was standing in the middle of the room, telling them all about my grandfather, Jock Stewart, and what a great piper he was. She quoted the epitaph that she had written for him.

Epitaph to Jock Stewart

It's of a poor but honest man
These words I sit and write,
He was not an educated man,
But a genius within his right.

For he mixed with lords and ladies,
And folk of high degree,
He also travelled the country round,
A life that was hard but free.

He was Scotland's greatest piper,
He held that title for many a year,
And to listen to his piping,
People came from far and near.

He took part in all the gatherings,
From Dundee to John o' Groats,
And there was never a piper in all the land,
Could ever compare his notes.

He competed with all the champions,
And was never at a loss,
With MacColl, MacLennan and many more,
Including Willie Ross.

When I think about the things he did,
It makes me stop to think
Of the vast amount of talent,
That was born in a tink.

He taught many pupils in his time,
Including Hugh MacMillan,
And to pipe him to his resting place
Hugh was more than willing.

But I saw a tear come to his eye,
As they lowered him to the ground,
And many hearts were breaking,
As they heard that haunting sound.

My mother received a great ovation for that. Then my father started to play the bagpipes. He played 'Lady Elspeth Campbell', 'Kintara to El Arish' and 'The Top of Craigvienin', my grandfather's tune. After that it was the hostess's turn: she played guitar and sang. She had a good voice, and her husband came in with the fiddle. The MP who had driven me back was next. He sang an old English ballad, but it had no story to it. He wasn't a very good singer either, but he did his best.

We stopped the party to eat and had a wonderful spread laid out in front of us. We all tucked in.

The next day, at about nine o'clock in the morning, we headed home. It took us ten hours.

We were exhausted when we got back. I came home to an argument as usual, but when I gave Ian the money he cheered up and that stopped the argument.

A couple of months later I fell pregnant again. We wanted a big family, but my mother wasn't too happy about the situation, and neither was my doctor. I was having my babies too quickly, according to the doctor, especially after being ill with TB.

There were no scans in those days, so we didn't know what sex the baby was, but I longed for a wee girl. Nine months later, in a bedroom of my parents' house, my prayers were answered, and I got my wee girl. My Heather was born on a Sunday, just as I was born on a Sunday. She was born with a lucky cap (part of the caul on the head of the baby which gives good fortune in later life), but the silly nurse threw it away. The doctor was furious with her, as I should have been given it. I also was born with a lucky cap which my granny kept for me.

I got the shock of my life just after the birth when the doctor came in and said to me that the ambulance was at the door.

'What for?' I asked.

'You are going to Dundee Infirmary to be sterilized,' he replied. 'Your husband and your mother signed the form giving permission for the operation.'

My wee girl was only half an hour old, and I was whipped away to the hospital. I was so angry that I had no say in the matter of my own body that I wouldn't speak to Ian or my parents. After a while I calmed down. I was used to my life's decisions being made for me, and so I just accepted it.

While I was in hospital for the operation, Cathie took Heather to stay with her. She lived in an old bus in my father's yard. My mother looked after the two boys.

A week later I was allowed home, and Ian persuaded me that sterilization was the right thing to do. The thing I had wanted to do more than anything was to breastfeed my wee girl Heather, because I had never breastfed the boys, but by the time I came out of the hospital she was on the bottle and I had no milk. I was so sad about that.

Heather was a wee doll and a good baby. My sister Cathie didn't want to give her back when I came out of the hospital.

15
Potato-lifting

A while after that it was the potato-lifting time. My father always had a squad going, and Ian and I would go along. The money was good, so even though I had three kids I still had to work. Having children then didn't keep the travelling woman from doing her share. We had wee Ian walking about the field, Hamish was in a scull (basket) and Heather was in the pram.

Ian and I always took three bits (areas of the field) between us, and Ian would measure them out before we started. He would light a fire at the end of one of the bits and keep it going. The people we had working for us were all travellers, so we boiled kettles on the fire to be ready for dinner-time. I used to work in the end bit near the fire, because it was cold weather, and it helped me and the kids to keep warm.

Dinnertime was an hour of laughing and just being travellers. We would make up rhymes as we were sitting round, rhymes that only travellers would understand, but I have decided to tell you a couple. Here is one that caused us all to collapse in laughter. It was started off by a traveller boy named Hughie, who said:

> There was an old man from Glengarry,
> He was eaten by an overgrown parry [louse].

This was our humour, and we laughed and laughed. The next contribution was:

> Sic a man was never born
> Like the shepherd o' the thorn,

He shot wee doggies just for fun,
Wi' a double barrelled gun.

The shepherd hadn't really shot any dogs, it was all make-believe. We would sing round the fire and tell ghost stories. Some of the women got so frightened that they wouldn't go into the wood for a pee, and the ones with long dresses on just squatted down, like the older travellers always did in the past. My granny never wore knickers in her life, and that was the reason.

We would do the potatoes for about four weeks. It was hard work, but the dinner-times made it enjoyable.

At the weekends we would visit the travellers' camps and have a great time. All the old songs and stories would be brought out. Sometimes the real Jack (Jeck) tales were told, ancient stories that travellers kept alive. Here is one of my father's favourite Jack stories. It needs to be put in my book, as no one else tells it now.

Travellers called him silly Jeck. Jeck lived with his mother and father, and his father was a blacksmith. Jeck worked with his father on the bellows keeping the fire going. It was a lovely summer's day, hot and glorious. Jeck's mother came out to her man and Jeck, and suggested they had their dinner out in the sun, with sandwiches and fruit. 'Oh mother, that's a great idea,' said Jeck, 'I will look forward to that.'

At dinner-time, as sure as her word, she brought out a great spread. They settled down at the door of the smithy and leaned against the wee dyke that was there, and started to eat their fill of the goodies.

A wee while later, Jeck's father said, 'Jeck, look at the road, there is a man coming and he is on a horse.'

When the man approached, they saw that he was a real gentleman, with a silk shirt on, and dressed in wonderful riding clothes. He jumped off the horse, and when they looked at the poor horse it was a rickle of bones. They were sticking out of its skin, and its ribs were protruding through its sides. The man asked in a very posh voice, 'Blacksmith, can I borrow the biggest, best hammer you have?'

'Of course, sir,' said the blacksmith, and pointing to where he kept his hammers hanging up, said to the gentleman, 'Take your pick, sir.'

The gentleman went over to inspect the hammers. He chose the biggest, best hammer in the bunch, and took the poor horse to the front of the smiddy, and he lifted the hammer and whacked it on the horse's back. You could hear its back breaking, and he kept hitting the poor horse and its blood was splattering everywhere. The horse was sinking with every blow that was struck, till it collapsed in a heap with its last breath.

Then a queer thing happened. The minute it gasped its last breath, a beautiful prancing stallion jumped out of the bones. The gentleman walked over to the blacksmith and said, 'Blacksmith, that is a wonderful hammer you have there. Take good care of it.'

He wiped the blood off it and hung it back in its spot. He then jumped on the horse and galloped away.

Jeck and his father watched him go with puzzled looks on their faces and scratching their heads, bewildered.

A while later the blacksmith said to Jeck, 'Jeck, did you see what that man did to the horse, and look at the great stallion that came out of the bones! You know, Jeck, our auld horse has seen better days, she is getting too old now to be much good to us. Jeck, that is a magic hammer. Well, you saw with your own eyes, didn't you?'

'Yes, Father, I did.'

'Well, go and bring the old horse from round the back, Jeck.'

'But Father, it's my mother's horse.'

'Never mind your mother's horse. When we get a big stallion she will be pleased.'

So Jeck went round the back, and brought the old horse to the door of the smithy, and it stood there all weary and old. The father had got the hammer and was waiting for Jeck to come back with old Bessy, the horse.

Well, the blacksmith lifted the hammer and hit the poor horse in the middle of its back, and you could hear its bones breaking. Jeck hid his eyes as his father continued hitting the horse. The last blow was in its forehead, and the blood splattered on Jeck's face. He rubbed it off in a fury.

When the horse had died, Jeck's father wiped the blood off the hammer, hung it up,, and waited, with arms folded, and waited, and waited and waited. Nothing happened.

After half an hour, Jeck started to cry about the poor horse, and said, 'Father, my mother will be so angry she may use the hammer on us.'

'Quick, Jeck, go round the back and get the old tarpaulin. We will wrap it in that and put it in the bog, and she will never know.'

So Jeck went for the tarpaulin, and raked what was left of the old horse into it, all the shattered bones and the blood, and trailed it round to the bog, and dropped it in. There was a sucking, plopping noise as it sank to the bottom.

Two days later, they were in the blacksmith's shop when Jeck's father looked up the road, and coming down on a horse was this same gentleman again. He nudged Jeck to look up the road to see him as well. The horse pranced down the road, and on the horse with the gentleman was a wee, withered woman. She had such sharp features you could crack nuts between her nose and her chin.

The gentleman stopped at the door, jumped off the horse and lifted the prune of a woman down off the horse. He walked over to the blacksmith and said, 'I have come, blacksmith, to borrow your wonderful hammer again. May I?'

Bewildered, the blacksmith just nodded his head, and the gentleman took the same hammer, and stood the old lady at the door of the smiddy and got her into position. Then he lifted the hammer, and with all his might brought it down on the old woman's body. Crack! Crump! You heard every bone in her body shatter, and there was blood all over the place.

When he gave her the last hit on her brow, she fell dead at

his feet, and within a few minutes, out of the bones jumped a beautiful creature. It was the most beautiful woman Jeck and his father had ever seen.

The gentleman wiped the blood off the hammer, and said, 'Guard that hammer well, blacksmith. Thank you.' He took the lovely creature and placed her on the horse, jumped on himself and galloped away.

Jeck's father looked at him and said, 'You know, Jeck, your auld mother is getting very old now, and she has seen better days.'

Jeck jumped up angrily and said to him, 'No, Father, don't even think of it. My poor mother!'

'Jeck, think about it, my son. A beautiful damsel coming out of your mother's auld weary bones. Son, we could share her.'

'No, no, Father, I don't agree.'

But Jeck being a silly boy, his father soon got round him, and he went into the house to tell his mother his father wanted to speak to her.

Out she came with flour all over her hands, because she was baking, and she wasn't too pleased at being called outside. The blacksmith had the hammer at his back so she didn't see it. She was standing at the door of the smiddy, helpless.

He walked up to her, and swung the hammer and hit her on the head with it, and he kept hitting her until blood and snotters were everywhere. Then she finally died.

He wiped the hammer and he and Jeck stood together watching, and watching and watching. Nothing was happening. They stared down at her bones, but no young woman came out of them. 'Father, it didn't work. What are we going to do now?'

'Jeck, go round the back and get the other tarpaulin, and we will put her in it, and put her in the bog beside the auld horse.'

So Jeck did as he was told, and he put her in the bog.

Jeck couldn't sleep all night thinking of his mother, and when he came down in the morning he had a wee bundle of clothes with him, and some bread and cheese. He came to his father and said, 'Father, I am leaving and never coming back. What you did to my poor mother was terrible, so I am leaving you, and I never want to see you again.'

Off he sped, walking more quickly than he had ever done before. He wanted to put as many miles between himself and his father as possible. He walked for miles and miles, till he came to a big gate, and he sat down to eat his bread and cheese. He had noticed a poster pinned to the gate, but Jeck couldn't read.

Then a man came past, and he said to the man, 'Could you read this notice to me, sir?'

'Of course,' said the man. 'It says, any man who can cure the king of his illness can have half his kingdom and his daughter's hand in marriage.'

'Thank you, sir,' said Jeck.

He thought for a while and said to himself, 'I could perhaps cure him.'

So he opened the gate and went up to the castle. He rapped on the door, and a butler came out.

'Well, my man, what can I do for you?'

'I have come to try and cure the king.'

'Well,' said the butler, 'many have tried and failed, from all over the world, but come in and I will tell His Majesty you are here.'

Jeck was shown into the throne room, and there sat the king with a huge blanket over his head. The king said, 'I hear you have come to try and cure me.'

'Well, sire, yes, I want to have a try at it.'

Just then the king took off the blanket and showed his head to Jeck.

Jeck jumped back when he saw it, and thought to himself, 'Oh my God!'

The king's head had a big, big, yellow, watery scab all over the top of his head.

Jeck walked round the king, examining it carefully.

'What is your verdict, my man?' said the king.

'Yes, sire, I believe I can cure you. Give me four of your

courtiers with four buckets and spades, and a bucket and spade for me.'

So the king supplied Jeck with what he asked for. 'Now,' Jeck said to them, 'We will go down to the field where the cows are, and we will collect all the cows' shit into the buckets, but try and get pats which are newly laid and still steaming.' So they filled up their buckets of cows' manure and went back to the castle with the full buckets.

They entered the throne room, and Jeck asked for a big, big piece of muslin. It was brought to him, and Jeck opened it out and spread the contents of the buckets on it.

'Now,' he said to the men, 'each of us will take a corner of the muslin, and we have to swing it and plop it onto the king's head.'

This they did. Then Jeck said to the king, 'Now, Your Majesty, you have to sit like that for 24 hours. Don't move. I will be back after 24 hours.'

Jeck was taken away to meet the queen and her daughter, a beautiful princess.

Twenty-four hours passed and Jeck and the four men entered the throne room. The king was in some mess. Green stuff was running out of the king's head onto the floor, and the smell was something terrible. The men were nearly being sick.

They each took a corner of the muslin, and with a jerk peeled it off quickly, and thumped it on the floor. When they looked at the king his head was as pink as a baby's bum, and the scab was stuck to the muslin. The king jumped up off the throne and danced a jig.

The wedding was set for the next day, and everything was got ready for it. And just as the minister was saying 'I now pronounce you man and . . .' Jeck's mother said, 'Come on, Jeck, you've slept long enough, get back to work.'

It was all a dream.

One night we were sitting round the camp-fire when a woman came into the camp and started shouting, 'Where's the boss, where's the boss?' Everybody was stunned at her arrival and her shouting. They all pointed to my father.

She ran over to him and knelt down in front of him. 'Can I have a job at your tatties?' she asked. 'I have no accommodation, but if there is a single man in the camp I don't mind sharing with him.'

My father looked at her, then looked around the fire at the other travellers, with a bit of devilment in his eyes. 'Oh, we have plenty of single men in the camp. I will line them up and you can take your pick.'

Everyone had to keep from laughing out loud. They knew my father was a joker, and always went along with his tricks. All the men around the fire stood up in a straight line, even my father. The women had to swallow their laughter.

Before the woman could choose, a voice from outside the firelight said, 'I'll take her.'

Looking around, the travellers saw Willie, a wee, thin, peely-wally looking man. He wasn't an ugly creature, but he had a couple of slates missing. Everybody knew that Willie had never had a woman in his life, and was still a virgin.

When the woman stood up and saw him, a big smile came over her face. 'I'll take you,' she said. She walked over, took him by the arm and they both walked off.

'Well, did you ever see anything like that,' said my father, bursting out laughing. Everyone laughed.

After that, no one saw Willie for four days, and he didn't go to his work at the potatoes. When he appeared on the fifth day, there was a smile across his face as big as Loch Ness. He was in a daze.

After the potato-lifting came the harvest. Ian and my father wouldn't let me help with the stooking once I had the kids, as it was a dangerous place for children, so I didn't go to the harvest,.

My father got a dog, a lurcher, for the bairns. He was a great dog. We named him Silver.

After we got the dog, Ian got a job in a jute mill as an oiler of the machines. We also got a house with the job at three shillings and sixpence a week, so we moved in. We were all in one room and the kids hadn't much room to play. I hated it there and missed our council house. A good job the children were small at the time.

16
On the Move

❧

My father bought a property in New Alyth, five miles from Blairgowrie. There were five houses in the block. We got one, Cathie got one and my mother and father moved into the largest one. A cousin of my mother got the fourth one and a Glasgow family got the final one. It was great to get away from that tiny mill house.

My girl Heather was about five when Gregor came along, in 1964. He was our pride and joy. We had longed for years for another baby and now we had one.

I took him along to see my uncle Donald who wasn't well at all. He was in his bed, but he held Gregor and cuddled him, kissing his brow. On Christmas Eve of that year, at five o'clock in the evening, my uncle Donald passed away. That was one of the hardest days of my life; to me it was the end of an era. A week later, on New Year's Eve, my mother's other brother, uncle Andy, died at exactly five o'clock. I had lost my two uncles within a week. Our family was devastated, and my mother was heartbroken, we had to comfort her a lot. These uncles had been the heads of our family all my life. They are both buried in Alyth churchyard.

I am so proud and glad that they taught me all their songs and ballads, and about their way of life. They left me with a great legacy. It is priceless.

We settled down again in New Alyth. My three kids went to Alyth primary school. We had many, many visitors coming to see us. One in particular was the well-known Dundee singer, Jim Reid. My family took him into their hearts, and we classed Jim as the best singer in Scotland. He became part of our family, an adopted son, as my mother would say. To this day Jim is still my favourite singer, he has that special conyach, a feeling for the music. He is just like a brother to me.

In July next year we had travellers to stay out the back in our garden. What a time we had. We picked berries all week, but had ceilidhs every weekend. On a Saturday our house was always full of music, singing and stories. It was so special, a time I don't think any folk-singer from that era will ever forget.

Jimmie, Cathie's man, and Ian got a job up at Glen Isla. They were building a dam up there. My sister Rena got a job as secretary on the site. They flooded part of the glen called the Strong Grips, or at least that's what the travellers called it. It used to be a great glen for hawking, but that disappeared with the dam. It was so good for Ian to be working again.

The job up the glen was soon finished, and Cathie and Jimmie went down to London, where they had just started building the Victoria Line. Jimmie did concreting and got a job no bother. They found a flat in Stamford Hill above a launderette. Two weeks later they asked us to come down, so off we were again to London. We stayed with Cathie for a week, then got our own place in Stoke Newington, just round the corner from Cathie. We paid six guineas a week for a three-bedroomed house looking over the park, which was a great place for the kids to play. Ian got a job on the Victoria Line as a joiner. He was the gaffer, with a squad under him.

A couple of weeks later my mother and father came down to stay with us because they had a few gigs in London. Then after another week my brother Andy came down, got a flat and his wife and father-in-law joined him. Andy only stayed two weeks, as the house he was staying in stank of paraffin, which they said was put on the floors to protect them. They left London and hadn't even done any work, so it was a holiday for them. A month later we came home with my mother and father, back to New Alyth. It was good to be home, but we had liked living in London.

We settled back down in New Alyth, but then my father

decided to sell the block of houses we were in – I think he sold them to the council, but I'm not sure. Where were we to go now, was the problem.

Ian decided to squat in a downstairs flat in Reform Street, Blairgowrie. My father took him along to the house, and he broke in with a crowbar.

We moved into the place that night. It had a living room and a bedroom, and was very basic, with the toilet outside. The police arrived, but when they saw who we were, they didn't bother us. The kids all went to school from there.

One day a traveller woman who was living up the road knocked on the door. 'Sheila,' she said 'I want to complain about your son Gregor. He beat up my grandson, and I am not going to stand for it.'

Standing beside her was a boy about 11 years of age. 'Are you sure it was Gregor?' I asked. 'Yes, I'm sure.'

I went in and brought Gregor out. He was three-and-a-half at the time. 'Well,' I said, 'here is Gregor.'

She looked at Gregor and said to her grandson, 'Is this him?'

'Yes, Granny, that's him.'

She took her grandson by the ear and dragged him off, shouting back to me, 'Sorry, Sheila, I am shamed to death for bothering you.' He got a good telling-off, I bet, and maybe a sore arse as well.

The council came to see us a week later. We had been squatting in the flat for a year at that time. They told us we were getting a council house at Ferguson Park in Rattray. We were so happy at the news. The house had three bedrooms, a kitchen and living room, and, to our joy, a toilet and bathroom inside.

We settled down fine in our new home, and Hamish Henderson came back to do more recordings. We went over to my parents' house three nights on the trot, recording. The first night my father told Hamish a great story about something that happened to him near Edinburgh, a good few years before, and this is how it went.

When My Father, Alex Stewart, Met the Burkers

Travelling folk had to watch themselves, because the burkers were always after them. Burkers were body-snatchers, and they were always trying to capture travellers. If they were caught, they had a chloroform cloth put over their mouth, and were never seen again. We lost a lot of family this way. The bodies were sold to the hospitals for science.

Me and my sister Jeannie were near Edinburgh, hawking tinware, basins, pea-strainers, all that kind of thing. We were getting closer to the city. I was taking one house and Jeannie was taking another, and we were selling a lot of stuff.

It was getting gloaming dark, but we could still see what we were doing. I said to my sister, 'Jeannie, we will have to try and get back to the camp before darkness comes upon us.' We were about three miles from the camping ground.

'Aye,' said Jeannie. 'We will have to run part of the way, although I am dead tired.'

So we were running on the road, and running on the road, when we heard the sound of a vehicle behind us. We looked back, and there chasing us were the burkers. They were just about two or three hundred yards away.

I saw a house nearby, a farm-steading. 'We had better go there,' I said.

We ran into the farmyard, and saw a haystack at the side of a field. 'If we get to the top of this stack, and bury ourselves into it, they won't find us,' I said.

We got on top of the haystack, made a hole right in the middle of it and got inside. Then I made a small hole on one side so that I could see out.

The car came right into the steading. Two men and two dogs got out and started to walk round the stack.

'Be quiet now, Jeannie, they're coming.'

The men had stopped walking about, but the dogs were still sniffing round the stack. We could hear the men saying, 'They must be around here somewhere.'

I put my hand in my pocket and took out my penknife. I opened the blade and stuck my hand with it through the small hole. One of the dogs started sniffing it. I put my other hand out of the hole, caught the dog's tail, and with one big swipe I cut the tail off the dog. The dog started to yelp and took off across the field with the other dog in tow.

The men were shouting, 'They are crossing the field, come on, we must run and catch them,' and off they went. Jeannie and I got out of the haystack and never stopped running till we got home to the camp. It was a narrow escape we had that night.

And that's the end of my story, Hamish.

Hamish was delighted with this story, because it was about the burkers.

Hamish then asked my mother about our superstitions and traditions. He was interested in what had been handed down to us. My mother started to tell him some of them.

Traditions to do with luck

If you go out and see the new moon, never come in and tell anybody in the house that you have seen it, let them discover it for themselves. When seeing it you must say, 'God bless what I see, and God bless us all till the next new moon.'

Never go out with a bare head after twelve o'clock on a Hogmanay night or you will have bad luck till next Hogmanay.

Never look at a funeral through a window, that is very bad luck.

If you are pregnant and a funeral passes, you have to cover your face and walk three steps after the hearse. Do this and you will have a healthy baby.

Family cures

For a sore throat, pee on your own stocking and tie it round your neck. Leave it on all night. (I have done this, and it works. My sore throat was gone in the morning.)

For a whitlow or an abscess, make a poultice with soap and sugar, and within four hours it will burst.

To cure dandruff, rub paraffin into the scalp.

To cure a headache, soak a cloth in vinegar and put it on your forehead.

To soothe wasp and nettle stings, rub them with dock leaves.

Put the milk of dandelion stalks on warts, and they will disappear.

For a weak bladder, take a glass of gin, with nothing added to it.

Just then a knock came to the door, and my father answered it. It was a traveller man and a wee child. The man was bleeding heavily, and the wee girl had scratches to her face.

'Come in, come in,' said my father, who knew the man. 'What the hell happened to you, Joe?'

'Oh, Bidley [this is what the travellers called my father], you have tae help me,' Joe replied. 'I don't ken if Jean is still alive or no'. We heard this noise outside our tent. The cover was lifted, and four police came into the tent and started hitting me with a truncheon. Then they dragged Jean out of the tent by the legs, and said she had robbed a house nearby. They coshed her a few times because she was screaming holy blue murder. Then there was silence – she must have passed out. I grabbed wee Maggie's hand and ran tae your hoose. Maggie's face was torn wi' the bushes scraping her face as we went through them.'

He collapsed into a chair. When my mother came with a cup of tea, he drank it down in one gulp.

Just then we heard the sound of an ambulance passing my father's house. 'That will be Jean going to the hospital,' said Joe.

'Come on,' said my father. 'We will go to the hospital and see what's happening.'

My father and Joe were gone for about an hour, and when they came back Joe was beside himself with grief. Jean was dead. Wee Maggie was screaming and saying, 'My mammy, my mammy,' over and over again. The look on Hamish's face showed he was devastated, as we all were.

'Where is she?' asked my mother.

'She's in the mortuary of the hospital,' said my father.

The recording session was over for that night.

My mother and father looked after wee Maggie for a few weeks afterwards. The police got off without charge. They were doing their duty, the court said.

Joe was a poor man, and only had a tent to live in. I will let you into a secret. My father and Hamish paid for the funeral, and they got the cords to lower his wife's coffin down into the grave. That was another reason we loved Hamish, he mucked in with anything that was needed at the time. Joe certainly needed the help my father and Hamish gave him and Maggie that day. Of course Jean was buried in a pauper's unmarked grave.

My father let Joe and Maggie live in their tent at the back of my parents' house for another two months, then they moved on.

17

The US Bicentennial

Ian, my oldest son, got married and moved out, and Hamish had a steady girlfriend. I got a letter from London asking me if I would represent Scotland at the American Bicentennial celebrations in Washington. I can tell you Ian wasn't happy about this at all, but the boys ganged up on him and said, 'My mother is going, and that's that.' So I went.

There were seven or eight British participants. A Gaelic singer represented the Western Isles, I represented mainland Scotland, an Irishman represented Ireland, and the other representatives were English.

We got the plane from Glasgow to Washington, and landed on a very hot, sticky day. We were to stay at Georgetown University, and I was sharing a room with the Gaelic singer. When we arrived at our room, there was a strange noise coming from outside, and when we looked out of the window there was a group of Indians doing a war dance, as we thought. We were terrified. The only time we had seen Indians before was in cowboy films in the picture house. We closed the curtains and lay down on the bed with our heads under the covers till all was silent.

The next day we had to go down to the Mall where we were performing. Every performer had to spend 15 minutes on each stage and there were over twenty stages. I did my first 15 minutes and headed for the next stage, where an old woman was singing. I stood in the wings listening to her. She was singing 'Barbara Allan'. Forgetting where I was, I said out loud, 'I ken that song!' When the lady heard my Scottish accent she invited me out on to the stage beside her. I went and sat down on a chair next to her, and we got started, one ballad after another, my version, then her version. A crowd began to gather, and we were mobbed with people. I forgot all about having to do my 15 minutes, and we spent an hour together. She was a wonderful person called Almeda Riddle, a very famous American singer from Arkansas.

That night I was late getting back to the canteen for my dinner. I was the last to arrive, and there was only one seat left – beside the Indian chief I had seen on that first night doing the war dance. I picked up my tray of food, and he shouted that there was a seat beside him. I went over and sat down. He was dressed up in his Indian regalia, and I was dressed in my Highland regalia. He had the feathers of his chief's head-dress right down his back and touching the ground.

We nodded to each other, and there was a big smile across his face. 'Hi, there,' he said. I said hi back.

We were wearing security badges with our names on them. Under his name it said Comanche Chief. He looked at me and asked, 'What do you do?'

I told him I was a Scottish traditional ballad singer from the travelling people of Scotland.

He looked puzzled. 'Travelling people, who are they?' he asked.

I started to explain that we were an ethnic group of people with a culture and a heritage of our own, and our own secret language.

'Mmm,' he said, 'did you say a secret language?'

'Yes, and it is not Scottish Gaelic,' I replied.

He considered for a while, and a funny look came over his face. 'I also have a secret language. It has to be kept alive through the men of the tribe, but I have forgotten where it came from. I have puzzled about it for years.'

I looked at him and said, 'If you tell me some words of your secret language, I will tell you some of mine.'

'Oh, no, I can't do that,' he answered.

I asked him why not.

He looked at me strangely and said, 'You are a woman.'

'So?'

'It is only the males in the tribe who are allowed to hear it,' he said. Then he glanced round the table to see if anyone was listening or watching, and he turned to me and spoke cant.

I looked at him in surprise and beamed. 'You said this food was crap, and you weren't going to eat it.'

He mumbled again. I laughed, and said to him, 'This coffee is crap and you aren't going to drink it.'

Well, he stood up and gave a whoop like a real Indian on the warpath would have done. I was petrified. But when he looked down at me there were two big tears running down his cheeks. His son came running over, and he spoke to him in the Comanche language. The son took my finger, then the chief's finger, and bound them together with a thin leather strap. He got his knife out, cut my finger and the chief's finger, and pressed them together.

'Now you are my blood sister,' said the chief.

'Why?' I asked him.

'You made me remember why we have to keep the secret language alive. Many generations ago, there was a man came over on a ship from Scotland. He tried to live with the Americans, but found that he couldn't. One day he was captured by some of my ancestors. Eventually he joined our tribe, fell in love with the chief's daughter and they married. He spoke funny, not like other Americans, and he said he was a tinker. He taught us many, many things about the earth, as well as tin-smithing and many more of his skills. The chief loved him like a son. When he died the most precious thing he left to us was his secret language. He had taught it to a few of the men in the tribe, because he missed his people, and wanted to speak in his own language with someone else. When he died, all the Comanche men had to speak his secret language in honour of his memory, and because he was a man the secret was kept in the male line.' The chief stopped speaking and smiled at me.

The next morning we were told we were to meet the Queen

and the Duke of Edinburgh at the Lincoln Memorial. We were all excited about it, especially me because it was my birthday, the 7th of July.

We arrived at the Mall with the other British participants. The Pearly Queen was to greet Her Majesty first as she came down the steps. I had on my full regalia of tartan, even a tartan tammy. The Queen walked down the steps, followed by Prince Philip. We were about 50 yards away from them. Her Majesty ignored the Pearly Queen and came right over to me. I was so embarrassed for the Pearly Queen. She took my hand and said, 'You are from Scotland, no doubt?'

'Yes, Your Majesty, I am.'

She smiled at me and said, 'Whereabouts in Scotland?'

'Blairgowrie,' I answered.

'Oh, I know Blairgowrie. We used to travel to Balmoral and go through Blairgowrie.'

'Yes, Your Majesty, you did, but not any more.'

'No,' she said. 'Well, if ever you are near Balmoral, do drop in for tea, Sheila.' (We had security badges, so she knew my name.) I nearly collapsed, and the only thing I could think of to say was, 'And if you are ever in Blairgowrie, do come in for tea also.' She nodded and smiled, and moved on.

Next, up came Prince Philip. He read my name and asked me what I did.

'I am a Scottish traditional ballad singer representing Scotland's travelling people, Your Highness.' The Duke turned to his security guard and said, 'Can we go down to the Mall to hear Sheila sing?' The security guard said, 'I am sorry, Your Highness, but security won't allow it.'

The Duke looked at me and said, 'F--- security!' and moved on.

I was so taken aback, but at that moment it struck me that royalty were human after all. I smiled to myself, thinking, 'Now I have heard it all!'

After the pomp and ceremony was over, we went down to the Mall to perform again. As before, it was 15 minutes each on stage after stage. We were so tired after a few hours, but finally got a break to go the food tent, to get something to eat.

I was halfway through my meal, when a tall man in dark glasses and a black suit came up to me and said, 'Are you Sheila Stewart?'

'Yes, I am,' I replied.

'Come and follow me,' he said.

I stood up and followed him. Another tall man joined us. He too had dark glasses on and a black suit. I was terrified. They led me to a long black car and told me to get in. I sat between the two men in the back seat and we drove off.

We drove for about 20 minutes, and pulled in at some big gates. I had to look twice. Oh my God, I thought, this is the White House. The car drove in round the back and parked. I was ushered out of the car and through a back door. We went along a corridor to two big double doors, and the two men opened them for me.

I couldn't believe my eyes. It was a huge room, and in it was the Queen, the US president Gerald Ford, his wife and ladies-in-waiting. Who should come over to me but Prince Philip. He took my hand and said, 'I told you I would hear you sing.'

Well, I sang, and then I had tea served, I may say, with pomp. The songs they liked best were 'Queen amang the Heather' and 'The Bonnie Hoose o' Airlie'. I spent two hours there, and at the end was shown back to the large black car. When I got into it, one of the tall men with dark glasses looked down on me and said, 'If you ever mention this visit to anybody, we will deny it.' I was shaking in my boots then, if I had boots on. As a result, I never told anyone about my White House visit for four years.

I got back to the Mall safely just as everything was packing up for the night. The bus was waiting for me, and I had it all to myself, as everyone else had already gone. I was late again getting to the dining room back at our accommodation. I opened the doors and everything was in darkness. I said loudly, 'Oh Ged! I have missed my dinner.'

Just like that, the lights came on, and standing there was my blood-brother, the Comanche chief, his wife and family, and all the other participants in the Bicentennial. My blood-brother held a huge birthday cake, and his wife had one as well. I was so surprised. After everything that had happened I had forgotten it was my birthday.

My blood-brother's wife had made me a ring in silver, with a blue stone, and he himself whispered, 'Sit down, and I will give you my present.'

We all sat at the tables, and he said, 'Now, Sheila, my blood-sister, my present is a story. You must keep it always and tell it wherever you go, and it will remind you of me.' He started to tell his story.

The Chief's Story

Indian tribes make up stories about nature, the wind, rivers and animals, and how things came about. Here is my story for you.

Away in a large forest, at the beginning of time, there was an animal. He was the most beautiful animal anyone had ever seen. He was pure white and fluffy, with a coat like angora wool. But he was also the vainest animal in all the world.

All day, every day, he would go to the pools in the forest to look at his reflection. He would preen himself and say, 'Oh, you are beautiful.'

One day, while he was preening himself, he stopped and put his hand to his stomach, and said, 'I'm hungry.'

He walked off to look for his dinner. He was walking through the forest when he caught a glimpse of an owl passing overhead.

'Ah,' he said to himself, 'if that's an owl there must be chicks in the nest up that tree. That will do for my dinner.'

The beautiful creature started to climb up the tree, and when he got to the nest, sure enough there were four chicks in it. He rubbed his paws together and said again, 'My dinner!' He put his front paw in and lifted up a chick by the scruff of the neck. The beautiful creature looked at it, turning it around, and said,

'My God, but you're ugly. If I eat you, you may blemish my beauty. You're too ugly to eat.'

He put it back in the nest, climbed down the tree and went off through the forest. Five minutes later, the mammy owl came back and the chicks were very upset. 'What's wrong with you?' asked the mother owl.

'Oh,' said the owl chick, 'There was a beast came up the tree, and grabbed me by the scruff of the neck, and said I was ugly, too ugly to eat. Surely I'm not ugly, Mammy.'

'Not at all,' said the mammy owl. 'What did this creature look like?'

'Oh, he was the most beautiful animal we have ever seen. His coat was like angora wool, white and soft,' said the wee chick.

'Ah, I know him,' said the mother owl. 'I will be back in ten minutes, so lie low,' and off she flew.

She flew all over the forest till she spotted the beautiful animal. She swooped down and picked him up by the scruff of the neck, flew to a part of the forest that was a raging fire, went into the middle of it and dropped him in.

She roosted nearby with her wings folded, waiting and listening to him scream. When she thought he had had enough, she swooped down and plucked him out of the fire by the scruff of the neck. She put him down on the ground and looked at him. Right down the right-hand side of his body was burned pure black, and down the left-hand side of his body was burned pure black.

The chief looked at me at this point and said, 'What animal is that, Sheila?'

Before I could say anything, a person from one of the other tables shouted, 'A skunk!'

The chief said to me, smiling, 'Sheila, that is the story of how the skunk was created. Now it is your story.'

I hugged him and his wife, and I said to myself, this is the best day I have ever had. We had a wonderful time that evening and it is a birthday I will never, ever forget.

The next day I was asked to stay on for another week to go

on tour, but I couldn't. Just before I left, my daughter Heather had had a wee baby boy. My husband got to name him, and called him Rob Roy MacGregor. I was desperate to get home to him and I missed all my family. So I returned immediately.

18
A Death in the Family

❧

I got home and was so glad to see my family – even big Ian kissed me. Mind you, I came back with money. I had only been away for ten days and it seemed like a month.

The weekend after, my father came up to my house and asked if I wanted to go and rake the Dunkeld dump. That was another thing we did to make money. We would get a lot of scrap in the dumps. Today you would call it recycling.

When we arrived at the dump, there was an old woman there sitting on an upside-down bucket with her clay pipe in her hand. Her two sons and her man were raking the dump and already had a pile of scrap, which my father bought from them.

The old woman called to me, 'Hi, lassie, come over here, will you?'

I went over and she said to me, 'Give me your finger.'

I held my forefinger out to her. She grabbed it and held on tight, then she stuck a pin in it and squeezed out the blood. Taking her clay cutty pipe, which was broken, she put the blood on the broken edges of the shank, and stuck the pipe together as if the blood was glue. This was what my granny did all the time to fix her pipe, but she used her own blood. It was the first time my blood had been used as glue, but I didn't say anything because we never spoke back to our elders.

All my father said was, 'The auld vampire needed some of your blood,' then he laughed his head off.

We went back to their camp to get more scrap from the travellers, and this time the old woman hugged me.

A week later Ian came home one night and said he had a job, on the pylons again. This was great news.

He started work on the Monday. Heather was away down to the nurses to have baby Roy weighed, and I was still in bed. I heard a rumble downstairs. I pulled my coat on and went down to the sitting room. There was a man standing in the middle of the floor, who had just climbed in the window. I knew who he was, so I didn't scream – he was a sheriff's officer. 'What are you doing here and what do you want?' I asked.

He replied, 'You are Mrs MacGregor?'

'Yes, I am,' I said

'Well, you owe some debt, and I have come to price your furniture to put it towards what you owe.' Then he started to price my television and my bits of furniture, one by one.

'You won't get much for my stuff,' I said, 'because I got it all free from the welfare in Perth.' I sat down in one of the chairs. 'What is this debt I owe, anyway?'

'It is a clubby book [mail-order catalogue],' he replied.

'A clubby book? I never had a clubby book in my life.'

'Well, it is in the name of Mrs MacGregor, and it gives this address.'

'What are the initials of this Mrs MacGregor?'

When he told me, the penny dropped. It was Ian's brother's wife, who had been using my address for the bills and getting the goods delivered to her own address.

When I explained the situation to the man, he apologised.

'That won't save you,' I said. 'You went to school with my husband Ian, and when I tell him you came into the house through the window, you have had it, boy.'

I may say Ian did get hold of him later, but what happened then he wouldn't tell me.

I waited my time, and when my sister-in-law came through the door, I made a dive at her. I was chasing her round the couch. I got one punch into her face before she fled out the door. Two days later she came back to the house as if nothing had happened. I didn't mention anything about it either, so we were friends again.

When my mother and father sold the block of houses in New

Alyth, they bought two adjoining houses on Yeaman Street in Old Rattray, where my uncle Donald used to live years before.

One morning I went over to see them. As they weren't up, I put the kettle on and made their breakfast, and took it up to them in bed. I asked my mother, 'Why are you not up this morning? You're usually up before this.'

'Oh, Sheila, don't speak, we weren't in bed all night,' she said. 'At about two in the morning a knock came to our door, and your father answered it. It was Davie in a terrible state.'

'Big Davie?' I asked.

'Yes, Big Davie. His wife Ninny and his family are staying along the road in two bell tents. Well,' said my mother, 'Ninny was with him, crying like mad, "Oh, Belle, help me, the pain is terrible." "What's wrong wi' you," I said. Her eyes were rollin' back in her heed. "Oh, Belle, there is an eariwig in my ear. It must have crawled in when I was sleeping."'

My mother phoned the doctor and he came up in about 15 minutes. 'He took some chloroform out of his bag and put some in her ear,' said my mother. 'He waited for a few minutes, and then he put a long instrument like tweezers in her ear. It had to go a good bit in, but he pulled the earwig out. Sheila, she collapsed with relief. Poor thing.'

'My God, mother, you certainly had a night of it.'

That was one thing about my family, there was never a dull moment.

My father said a funny thing to me that morning when he got up out of bed. He was a man who very rarely made a comment about anything, but this morning he did. 'Sheila, I was thinking and laughing to myself about the last few weeks. You were in America, met royalty, and were made the blood-sister of the Comanche chief. Then you come home and go raking a midden, and give your blood to an auld traveller woman to glue her clay cutty thegither. How do you feel about that, now?'

'Daddy, I was born a traveller and I will die one. I prefer travellers any day, they are my folk. I will never change.'

125

My mother looked at me and said, 'Well, there's one thing, you're no' stuck up, anyway. You're a good lassie, Sheila.'

A wee while later Big Davie came in with his two sons. He said Ninny was in her bed sleeping. He sat down and I made them all tea, and we had a good crack.

Hamish appeared again just before the berries were finished to do a bit of recording. A friend of ours, old Weenie Brazil was still there, and we had a great night. Hamish even recorded Weenie tap-dancing. I think the School of Scottish Studies must still have that tape.

Ian was so thrilled with Rob Roy he took him everywhere with him. It didn't keep him out of the pub altogether, but when he came home from work he would rather stay at home at nights and play with Roy as we called him. Roy was his pride and joy.

Even with Ian working, we couldn't keep up the payments on the rent for the house, so we had to do a moony (midnight flit). We headed up to Inverness with a caravan, and stayed on the banks of Loch Ness.

Ian got a job on a building site in Inverness, and we pulled our caravan up beside his job. We were there for a few weeks. One night Ian went out drinking with some of his co-workers. Time wore on, time wore on, and there was no sign of Ian coming back from his night out. At four in the morning a knock came to the caravan door. I opened it, and there he stood, covered in blood. He could hardly get up the step of the trailer, and I had to help him in. Everyone was awake by this time. His lips were so swollen, we couldn't make much sense of what he was saying. My Heather got a terrible fright, as we all did.

He slept on the bunk that night. I couldn't wash the blood off his face as it was still too sore. In the morning he was still sleeping; it was a good job it was Sunday, and there wasn't any work.

I said to Heather that morning, 'I hope he still has his wages. He won't have them all, but surely he didn't drink them all.'

When he woke up, he sat up and looked at me very coy-like. 'Sheila, I got robbed last night by a taxi-driver. I asked him to take me home, but instead he took me in the opposite direction. He pulled me out of the car. I was paralytic drunk and couldn't save myself. He gave me this hiding, and knocked me into a ditch. I must have been there for a few hours, unconscious. Then I crawled out of the ditch and came home.'

What a face he had, he was unrecognisable. My Heather has a traveller's sense of humour. She looked at him and said, 'Dad, you look like Quasimodo, the bell-ringer.' We all burst out laughing.

I really had not much sympathy for him. We had not a penny to our name. Ian couldn't work in the state he was in, so we would have to go home, but we had no money for petrol.

The next morning I went onto the building site and told Ian's boss what had happened. He said he would come up and see him. When he looked at Ian, he grimaced. 'Here, Sheila, here is money for petrol to get you home. You can send it back to me.' He gave me £20, which meant we could also eat on the way down.

I drove all the way down and then stopped at a lay-by near Dundee. The next morning we went to Totie's house, where we got a meal from his wife. We put our name on the council list for a house, and got one after a week at Mid Craigie in Dundee.

We were happy in Dundee, because Ian had no pals to go to the pub with, and only went for a pint when we went for our shopping.

Gregor and Roy were still at home with Ian and me. Young Ian and Hamish stayed in their own houses in Whitfield, and Heather was married, and living in Coupar Angus.

It was now 1977. As usual we went through to stay with my mother and father in Old Rattray to do the berry-picking. This was the only time of the year we had money – not plenty of money, but we always had food on the table.

Before we left Dundee to go to Old Rattray, Ian and I bought Totie his 21st birthday present. We bought him a radiogram. It was left in Dundee till his birthday on 8 August. The day before his birthday, we decided that Big Ian would go to Dundee on the bus to pick up the radiogram, and my mother, me, Gregor and Roy would go along to New Alyth to pick berries.

Ian came back on the bus that night and had his tea. Then he said to me, 'Sheila, have you any cigarettes?'

'No, I was just going to the shop to buy some.'

So we both got into the car and headed down to Blair for cigarettes. I was driving, and I could see Ian was very tired. He was nearly falling asleep. After we had been to the shop, we were passing the Wellmeadow in the car when one of Ian's mates saw us and hailed us down. I didn't want to stop but Ian did. He rolled down the window and his mate spoke to him. 'Come on, Ian, we are going fishing the night.'

Ian said, 'No, I am far too tired. I have been in Dundee all day.'

But his mate wouldn't give in. 'Come on, we need you.'

I looked at Ian and said, 'You have been away all day, tell him no.'

'I can't, Sheila, but I won't be long,' and he stepped out of the car and walked away.

He didn't come home all night, and in the morning I was fuming because that would be another day he didn't go to the berries with us. That afternoon we were in the field when Gregor looked up and said, 'Mum, here comes the police doon our drill.'

I looked up and said, 'What's happened now?'

The policemen came up to me and said, 'Sheila, come with us.'

'Why?' I asked.

'We will tell you when you get home. Get your mother and the kids to come as well.'

We piled in the car and followed the policemen home. When we got out of the car, and before we went into the house, one of the policemen turned and said to me, 'Sheila, I am sorry, but Ian's body was found on the river bank this morning. He was found by two kids going to school.'

I was dumbstruck. The door opened and Cathie and her man Jimmy came out and brought me into the house.

'We went over, Sheila, and identified him. It is definitely Ian. But our word can't be taken as final, it has to come from you.'

I couldn't speak; it was as if I had lost the power of speech. A policeman then knocked on the door and came in. 'Sheila, you will have to come with us to identify the body.'

I got angry then, and said to myself, 'Body? What body?'

I followed them out to the police car, and we headed for the cottage hospital. The mortuary was round the back. Cathie came with me, for support. I entered the cold, damp building, just one big room like a concrete shed. A shiver went through me, and for a moment I wondered why I was in this place.

Then they took the sheet off his face, and Ian was lying there dead.

I started to scream, and threw myself at him, touching his face. But when I touched him, my hands jumped back as if there were springs attached to them. I had never felt cold like it. It was a clammy cold. My tears were dropping on Ian's cheeks. The policeman took my arm, led me outside and put me back in the car.

They dropped us off at my mother's house. I walked in and sat down on the armchair, and ten minutes later Hamish and young Ian walked in. They knelt down at my chair and cuddled me. It wasn't till I saw them that the reality of the situation sank in. When my Heather arrived, I felt so much better, why, I don't know. She was an angel to me that day.

I don't remember much about the time before the funeral. Ian and Hamish arranged everything. There was a post-mortem and they didn't let me have him for burial for over a week. All that time I ate nothing; I got it into my head 'Why should I eat when Ian isn't eating?' Then a bit of depression set in. I felt I couldn't go on. I have tried to remember the day of the funeral, but I can't.

A few weeks later I was asked to go to the coroner's office in Dundee to get the results of the post-mortem and the cause of Ian's death. On that night he had been in the water with waders on and slipped on a stone. The waders had filled up with water and dragged him down and he drowned. But in the post-mortem they discovered that the main artery going to his heart was completely shrivelled up, like a prune. He would have only lived another six months, at the most, anyway.

19

A Man You Don't Meet Every Day

❧

A couple of weeks after the funeral, me, Gregor and Roy went back to our house in Dundee, but I knew I couldn't stay there by myself. So we packed up, moved back to Blairgowrie and stayed beside my mother and father. My father had bought two houses in Yeaman Street. My parents were living in one, so we moved into the other next door. It was only one room, but it was a huge room, and fine for us.

A couple of weeks later there was a family meeting in the house. It concerned my father's sister, auntie Maggie. She had been in hospital and was due to come out. She was over 80 and a wee bit wandered.

All the members of the family at the meeting, her son, her daughter and cousins, said they couldn't look after her. No one wanted her. They argued for about an hour about where she was to go. I got fed up with them, and shouted at them all, 'I will take her! I will move into her house in Blair, me, Gregor and Roy. It's no problem for me to look after my aunt.'

Well, we moved into her house in Blair, and got it ready for her coming out of the hospital in Dundee. She came home in an ambulance, and was so pleased to see it was me that would be looking after her. She could be a cantankerous old woman, but I always got on fine with her. We entertained her every night before she went to sleep. I would speak about the old times to her. It made her laugh and cry, but she loved it.

It was two weeks before her son came to see her, and she didn't want him there. I warned her she had to behave herself when he was there. He stayed 15 minutes and she never spoke once to him. She was whispering all the time to me, 'Get this strange man out of my house.' When he had gone, I said to her that it was her son, not a strange man. She replied, 'I don't care if it was Rob Roy Macgregor, I don't want him in here.' I ran through to the kitchen laughing. In fact she did have Rob Roy staying with her.

One day I was bending over her bed tucking her in. She had a heavy glass ashtray in her hand, and when she turned in the bed the ashtray came down on my brow, splitting it open. She didn't know she had done it, and I did not tell her. I ran through to the kitchen, washed the cut and stuck a plaster on it.

That night her son and daughter came to see her, and noticed the cut on my head. When I explained what had happened, they would not believe me. They said she meant to hit me with the ashtray. No matter what I said, I couldn't change their minds. 'We are putting her into a home, Sheila,' they said.

'Why?' I asked.

'She is becoming violent with you, and needs to be taken away. The ambulance will collect her tomorrow.'

I looked at them, and said, 'You booked her into a home before you saw my head?'

'Yes, but that put the tin hat on it. She is going in to Murthly.'

'Murthly – but that's a place for the insane!'

'Yes, and that is what she needs. Have her clothes packed and get her ready for eleven o'clock in the morning.'

'I will not. You can do it yourself, because I won't be here to see my auntie Maggie be taken away to Murthly.'

I took the two kids and drove up to my mother and father's house to tell them. My father was livid, He went to see her son and daughter, but there was no changing their minds.

I stayed away that night, and waited till three o'clock the next day before I went back to the house. We packed up our belongings and went back to stay with my mother and father in

Yeaman Street. I did miss my aunt, and I bet she missed us as well. Poor thing.

A while after that, I was staying in a caravan in Sheffield, one time round about the early 80s. There were a lot of travellers there, and a job came up for a liaison officer to work with them. I applied for the job and got it. I was so excited; it meant that I could help to look after the travellers and to see fair play for them, something I always wanted to do.

The first day I went to the job I found out it covered Leeds and Bradford as well as Sheffield, and I wasn't just a liaison officer but also a social worker too.

The first case I dealt with was about three girls not attending school in Leeds. I went to the school to explain why; it was because the family was moving away from the area. I attended court cases where travellers were accused of theft, GBH and many other things. I also got social security benefits for travellers who didn't know how to get them. If they got any mail I had to read it to them and answer it for them. It was an exciting job, and I got on well with all the travellers down there.

The worst part of the job was evictions. I hated them. I had to be there when all the caravans were pulled off the land by police and councillors. It was a sad time for those getting evicted and for me.

I went to an eviction one day and was taken in by an old woman and given a cup of tea. 'Come in, dear,' she said, 'they are not here yet,' meaning the police.

Then she told me a horrendous story. I will tell it to you in my own words, and hope you can visualise it for yourselves.

It was a beautiful sunny day, and over beyond the bank near where their caravans were parked, Mary lay flat on her back. She was dreaming the kind of dreams that only a ten-year-old can dream. The sun was blinking through the trees and shining in her eyes, making her squint.

Mary loved the summertime as she and her family moved about from place to place working. They had arrived there two weeks earlier, and they were waiting for work to begin nearby. It was the first time they had stayed so long in one place without being moved on, and contentment reigned in the family.

Mary's granny had been ill now for a few weeks and was always in bed. She was sad every time she thought of her granny, saying to herself, 'what if my granny dies?' But she put that thought out of her head.

Just then there was a great noise from over the banking, with dogs barking, motors running and folk shouting. Mary crawled up the bank and peered over. Oh no, she thought, not again! and ran towards the commotion. Everyone was screaming and shouting and pointing to the roadway. There they were, the police coming to evict them again.

She recalled her granny's words: 'Mary, we are travelling people and we have a strong culture and a proud race. If we lived like the country hantle we would lose our identity, caged in a house all our lives.'

A scream pierced through Mary's thoughts. Mary's brother Jimmy started shouting at a very official-looking man. 'Please, sir, my granny has just died! Can't you wait till morning, then we will go?'

Mary couldn't believe what she was hearing. Granny dead? No, no, it couldn't be true.

Then she heard a sound she had heard many times before. When she turned around there was a great big beast of a tractor coming to drag the caravans off the site. Jimmy ran to the front of his granny's trailer and lay down in front of it to stop the iron beast from dragging it away, but the big tractor kept on coming. Jimmy, who was epileptic, then started to have one of his fits and couldn't move away anyway. A man from one of the other trailers grabbed him and pulled him clear.

Mary, by this time, was looking for her two wee dogs and put them in the back of her family's lorry. Then she heard a scream and looked to see that a policeman was dragging her

mother by the hair. Her father hit the policeman and he went
flying on his back. The whole family then jumped in their lorry
and headed out of the site.

Mary turned to her mother and said, 'Is it true granny's
dead?'

'Yes, my love, she passed away. But just think, my love, she
missed all this trouble and won't have to go through it ever
again.'

This really did happen, two years before I went to the area, and
it was typical of the kinds of evictions that travellers suffered all
the time.

Then I started back with my father scrapping and collecting
rags, anything to make a shilling. We collected brock wool
(scraps of wool gathered up from fields and fences) and fleeces,
and made a good lot of money. My father was the only traveller
to receive a licence from the Wool Marketing Board for brock
wool, and so we were allowed to collect it.

We also tried the mole-catching. We had a pump with gas in
it and pumped it down the mole holes. We got so much an acre.
My father didn't like the moling, so we didn't do it for long.

We always got a gig here and there singing, but that never
brought us in a lot of money. We also still did the outside work,
holing the berries, cutting them out and lacing.

My father couldn't do the outside work any more, because
he went to the hospital and was diagnosed with pernicious
anaemia. The white cells in the blood were taking over the red
ones, and he had to keep going into hospital for blood transfu-
sions. He would feel better for a couple of months, then he
would have to go back in for more blood. This lasted for a
couple of years, and I could see he was tired of it.

Myself and Cathie had a booking at the Waterside Festival in
England. The day before we were due to leave, my father got
taken into hospital very ill. I went in to see him that night, and
he didn't look well at all.

I said to him, 'Cathie and I won't go to this festival in England tomorrow.'

'Ah, but you must go,' he said. 'You know, Sheila, we have never let anyone down in our lives, and you will go. I'll be fine, and youse can tell me all about it when you come back. I will probably be home by then.'

So next day we headed for England in my father's car. We arrived late at night at our destination, where the festival was starting in the morning. It was a lovely day the next day. There was to be a concert at five o'clock that afternoon.

Directly behind the stage was a bar, and all the drink was on shelves backing onto the stage. We went into the bar, and Cathie said to the barman, 'Will the bottles be on the shelves like this when we sing tonight?'

'Yes, of course,' said the barman.

Cathie burst out laughing and looked at me.

'What's wrong with you?' I asked.

'You will be singing on stage while there's a bar through the wall from you,' and she burst out laughing again.

It hit home with me then. 'Well, you can tell them, because I'm not going to,' I said.

Cathie said to the barman, 'When Sheila sings, she will knock all the bottles off your shelves. Now, we are warning you beforehand!' The barman laughed and shook his head.

The concert started and two acts went on before us. Then we were on. We went on stage together, and Cathie sang first as she always did. Then it was my turn. I started singing, and after five minutes we heard banging and crashing from through the wall. Everything fell off the shelves, as it always does when I sing. Afterwards the barman said I was a nightmare, but we just laughed and said we did warn him.

We got home to our digs that night, and half an hour later the phone rang. It was my son Ian telling me my father had passed away. I cannot describe how we felt. Our world had caved in on us. I said to Cathie, 'Get in the car, we are going home now.'

The folk we were with tried to get us to stay till morning, but I was adamant that we had to get up the road. Cathie didn't drive, so I had to drive all the way home while Cathie slept. When we arrived at the door, I fell out of the car with exhaustion.

We headed for Ninewells Hospital, but when we got there my father was out of the ward and in the mortuary. 'I will not go to a mortuary to see my father,' I told Cathie and my son Ian. We made arrangements for him to come home to us the next day.

That afternoon we got a big shock. We were having a cup of tea when a knock came to the door and in came the minister from Rattray. He sat down on a window seat, looked at my mother and said, 'You know, Mrs Stewart, I cannot attend to your husband's funeral, because you were not members of my congregation.'

I spoke up then: 'But we tried to join your church many, many years ago, but you wouldn't let us in. Why was that?'

'You were travelling people, and we didn't want you mixing with our congregation.'

'So you won't bury my father?'

'No, I'm afraid not.'

We showed him the door. My mother started to cry then. 'Sheila, what are we going to do now?'

We spoke to a minister in Blairgowrie and he got a minister from Dundee. His name was Hector McMillan.

My father's remains came home the next day and we had his bedroom emptied waiting for him. All his family and friends came from all over Scotland to pay their last respects.

My sister Rena came down that night with her two kids, a boy and a girl. My father had adored them, as we all did. Travellers always take their kids to see dead relatives, it is part of our culture. Rena took them into the room where my father was lying in his coffin. It was just as if he was sleeping. Michael, my sister's wee boy, came out and said to his mother, 'Why is Da sleeping in his pipe box?' (The whole family called my father Da, and my mother Ma.) We couldn't help but laugh at what Michael had said. If you knew my father at all it was what you would think of.

My father was buried in Alyth cemetery, and his best pal, big Willie McPhee, piped at the funeral. The Rev. Hector McMillan gave a service as if he had known my father all his life.

When everybody was moving away from the graveside I looked back, and big Willie was looking down into my father's grave. I went over and heard him say, 'Goodbye, old pal. I might be with you soon.' He burst into tears. I gave him my hankie because he didn't want the rest of the mourners to see him crying.

I am grateful to him and all our friends, folksingers and musicians, for attending my father's funeral and paying their last respects. He was a man you don't meet every day.

20
Italian Tour

A week after my father's funeral I decided to take my mother away for a few days, and we headed up to Oban. On the way there, I saw smoke rising from a wee wood beside a stream. 'Look, mother,' I said, 'there are travellers camped over there.'

She looked over and said, 'Oh, Sheila, can we go over and see who they are?'

So over we went, and it turned out that the man, Geordie, was a cousin of my father's. They were so pleased to see us. They invited us to sit down at their fire, and they fed us mince and tatties and doughballs. The food was so good, made outside on the fire, there was a different taste to it altogether.

We had to leave them then and book into a hotel for a few days – so different from pitching up with our tent. We said we would go back and see them the next day. At three o'clock the next day we visited them again, and my mother took a bag of groceries to them.

We sat round the fire, had a bite to eat, then started to talk. Geordie said to my mother, 'You ken, Belle, Bidley [the name travellers called my father] was a great honest man. Many a time he helped me out when I was stuck.'

The woman, Bridget, took out her clay cutty pipe and asked if we minded her having a smoke.

'For God's sake,' said my mother, 'we're travellers tae, ye ken.'

So she lit up, and it was great to smell the pipe reek mixed in with the stick smoke. It reminded us of the past. My mother was in her element, sitting round a camp-fire speaking to travellers.

'Now,' said Geordie, 'I have a queer story to tell you. It happened to me and Bridget a couple of years ago.

One night we were sitting round the fire near Dundee, and it was gloaming dark. We heard a rustle of something coming towards us. We looked up and coming near the fire was a man. In the glow of the fire we could see he had a long black coat on. He was so tall we couldn't see his face properly.

"Come in near the fire and have a heat and a sit-down, stranger," I said. "Would you like a cup of tea?"

In a deep voice he said, "Thank you very much," and sat down. Now we could see him clearly. I nudged Bridget not to say anything. This man had the longest face we had ever seen. I guarantee you, Belle, it was over two feet long. He had big bolting eyes, his mouth drooped to the one side, one of his ears was nearly sitting on his cheek, and his face was baked with dirt.

"My name is Ben," he said in his gruff voice. "Long ago I used to walk this road all the time, but it became harder as I got older. I hid myself from everyone because of how I look. One day I covered my face and approached a travelling woman, and asked her to read my fortune. When she read it, she said that I was special. Then she grabbed the cover over my face and took it off. 'Oh my, my,' she said, 'you really are special. I can just tell you one thing, my man: kindness can only come from a tinker.' Then she walked away. So tonight I saw your fire and approached your camp.'"

'I just shook my head in acknowledgement,' said Geordie. 'He then asked us if we had any place he could kip down for the night. Bridget looked at me, and we were shaking with fear, but before I could say anything, Bridget spoke. "Well, I can give you a blanket and you can sleep under our cart." So she went to get the blanket. I followed her and said, "What the hell are you doing, Bridgie?"

"Well, I am so feart to refuse him, God knows what he might do."

We came back with the blanket, and asked him if he minded sharing his bed with our dog. He replied, "Not at all."

But when we tried to get that dog to go anywhere near him, we couldn't. So the dog slept in our tent at our feet. We finally fell asleep, and awakened next morning feeling refreshed. A glow came over us. Then we remembered the man. I jumped out of bed, and out of the tent, but there was no sign of the man. The blanket was there, and on the top of it lay the man's coat, just as if he had walked away and left it. We never saw that man again, and we packed up and moved on.'

'Oh my God above us, that was a terrible thing to go through,' said my mother.

'Aye, it was,' said Bridget.

'Now, Bridget,' said Geordie, 'come on and sing us a wee song to get us off the subject of Ben.'

Bridget sang two verses of a song about a drunken man fighting in a pub. I think they must have made the song up themselves, but it seemed to have no tune, and she couldn't remember anything but the two verses.

Well, we left them there and bade them goodnight, and said that we would be back the next day.

When we returned the next day, they were gone. 'They were a nice couple, and good company,' said my mother, and I agreed with her.

We went back to Oban to see Ganavan Sands where we all used to live, and spent another night in a hotel. Next day we headed back to Blairgowrie and reality, to try and cope with the loss of my father. But the getting away for a few days helped my mother no end.

One month after our wee holiday, we received a letter from Italy asking us to appear at a festival in Bologna. I thought to myself, 'This will get my mother back to the singing again.' So Cathie and me, my son Ian and my mother decided to go.

We had a good flight over to Milan where we got the train to Bologna. We got on the train fine, it was getting off that was a nightmare. When the train stopped, which it did for just a short time, we couldn't get off with folk pushing to get on. My mother was panicking. We were crushed like sardines, and they didn't care. We finally got off after a great struggle. My mother was exhausted.

Cathie and I and Ian couldn't help but laugh when we looked at my mother. She was all dishevelled, her hair was in a mess and her coat nearly hanging off. We should not have laughed, but we couldn't help it.

We arrived at the festival office to book in and be given the name of our hotel. We sat down and were introduced to the director of the festival. He shook Ian's hand and kissed us on the cheek. It turned out he was a great friend of Hamish Henderson, and used to work at the School of Scottish Studies in Edinburgh. He had met us before, though we couldn't remember him. We met so many collectors, we couldn't remember every one.

A girl appeared with coffee in small cups, and gave us one each. Well, you should have seen my mother's face when she took a sip, it was a picture. We all felt the same. She whispered to me, 'It tastes the same as the smell of your dad's old socks!' I burst out laughing, and couldn't stop. Ian and Cathie did not know what we were laughing at, but they found out later on.

A woman came in then and said, in Italian, that we were to receive one million lira each for our food and expenses. Cathie must have forgotten where we were, because she chimed up, 'We are millionaires!' You should have seen the smiles that came over our faces then. We didn't realise how little a lira was.

Another woman took us to our hotel. It was very basic but it was clean. Cathie, me and my mother shared the same bedroom, and Ian got a single room next door.

We had to buy our own food – that was what the million lira were for. There was a pizza café next door. Ian was desperate for a real Italian pizza, so we ate there. I can't remember what we ordered, but Ian ordered a large one. When Ian's pizza came, it was the biggest one we had ever seen, it was huge. Ian's eyes popped out of his head when he saw it. He ate a quarter of it and took the rest of it away in a doggy bag. I think he nibbled on it for a few days.

The next day we were taken to a village up in the mountains. The road we travelled on was the narrowest we had ever seen. On one side was big rocks, and on the other was a big chasm.

However, we got there safely. It was a quaint little place away on the top of a hill. We were taken to a bar across from where we were to perform. My mother ordered cherry brandy and so did I. Cathie had a beer and Ian had orange juice. The barman came with our drinks and the cherry brandy was in half-pint glasses. We looked at them in amazement. Cathie got a packet of cigarettes, and they were more expensive than the two cherry brandies. My mother said to me, 'I think I will stay here because the drink is so cheap!'

Eventually we were ushered to where we were to perform. It was an open-air stage built for us at the back of the mayor's residence. Half of the stage was suspended over a cliff. We had an interpreter with us to tell everyone what we were saying. Ian started with the pipes, and the whole audience started to dance, it was magic. People were streaming into the back yard. We performed our individual pieces, until we came to the last song, a bothy ballad, which we performed together. It was some finish!

We were mobbed at the end, it was fantastic the reception we received. We were told the whole village had turned out to see us.

Then we were ushered into the mayor's huge office. He was sitting there smiling at us. He could speak some English, and thanked us very much for entertaining the village. He said he had something to give us in appreciation of our performance. He produced five huge folders and gave us one each, with books to accompany them. He said, 'These are copies of prints from a collection of my paintings.'

He looked at me and added, 'You shall have the extra one, because you have such beautiful eyes.' So I got two folders. I don't know if Cathie or my mother were pleased, but I know I was. I don't think we will ever forget the trip we made to that village on the hill.

We got back to Bologna in time for dinner, and someone took us to a restaurant that served Scottish food. We were so pleased. We had broth, mince and tatties and apple pie. You can bet we went back to the hotel content that night.

We had been back home for a week when we got another letter from Italy. This time they wanted us to go to Lake Como for another festival in a week's time.

My mother said to Cathie, 'Will you dye my hair for me? I want it tinged with blue to take the greyness away.' It was all the rage then to dye hair blue. Cathie agreed, and said she would come up the next day to do it. That pleased my mother.

Next day Cathie came up and got ready to put the dye on her hair. 'I want you to do it in my bedroom,' said my mother, 'in case someone comes in. They would just laugh at me with blue dye on my hair.' So Cathie did what she was told.

I went down to the wee shop at the bottom of the hill to get the papers. On the way home I met someone and stood chatting to them for about 15 minutes. When I arrived back, I could hear Cathie on the phone in the kitchen. Where was my mother? I opened the bedroom door and there she was, screaming Cathie's name. When I looked at her hair, it was deep purple.

I went through to tell Cathie, and all she said was that the phone had rung and she had forgotten about the dye. She had left it on three-quarters of an hour, and it only supposed to be on for 15 minutes, so you can imagine what it looked like. 'Well, you had better go out the back door,' I said, 'because she is livid with you. Don't come back for a few days at least.'

I could not help laughing, in fact I was hanging over the sink in hysterics. I laughed so much that my mother started to laugh as well when she looked in the mirror. 'Stop it, Sheila, it's nothing to laugh at.' Then she started laughing again. 'Now, come on, Sheila, wash this dye off my hair.'

Little did she know, it wasn't that easy. It was permanent dye. I tried and tried, but I couldn't make an impression on it at all.

She pushed me away and said, 'Let me try.' Well, she collected Vim, bleach and kitchen cleaner. Anything you would use as a detergent, she put it on. Her scalp was red raw. The bleach helped a wee bit, but not much.

The day we were ready to go to Lake Como, Cathie appeared. She came in with her head down, apologising all the way into the living room. My mother had calmed down by this time and cuddled her, but said in no uncertain terms that never would she let Cathie near her head again.

21

Helping Travellers Out

A few days later we were in Lake Como. What a beautiful place
it was. We were worked hard there, and didn't have much time
to ourselves, but the day after we arrived we had the afternoon
off. We went to the square where everyone was congregated. It
was a huge square with many cafés in it.

Facing the square was the biggest church we had ever seen.
Cathie said, 'I want to go in there,' so we went up the huge
steps. It was unbelievable. There were statues of Jesus and the
Virgin Mary all over the place. In one corner there was a statue
of Jesus lying down on a slab. Cathie went over to look at it.
Just then we heard a terrible commotion going on, and when
we looked round Cathie was arguing with an old woman. We
went over and Cathie said, 'She is trying to push me out the
door, and pointing to my head and arms.'

Just then the church caretaker came up, grabbed the woman
and pushed her, screaming her head off, out of the door. He
finally got her out, and came back to speak to us. 'It is alright,
she is away now. She didn't want you looking at Jesus with
nothing on your head and bare arms. Enjoy the rest of your
stay.' We walked over to a café and got some coffee to calm
our nerves.

On a stage there was a band playing something that sounded
like pipes, but when we looked at the piper the bag he was
blowing was huge, I mean really enormous, and it didn't have a
cover on it. Ian went up to him and took out his Scottish pipes
to show them to him. Ian blew them up and started playing
and they wouldn't let him off the stage. He was playing one
reel after another, and everyone was dancing. Then Ian tried

the other man's pipes and the Italian blew up Ian's pipes. What a racket they made. Finally they stopped, laughing their heads off. The band asked us to come back the next day, but we said we couldn't as we were performing at the other square in the evening. They all said they would come along.

We arrived the next night, after being collected from the hotel. We were all fully dressed in Royal Stewart tartan. We really looked good. There was a small tent at the back of the stage which was our dressing-room. Soon the compère of the event came and said we had five minutes. Then we were ushered up some stairs on to the stage. When we got up there, we couldn't see a thing for the bright lights. We thought we had no audience. Ian started with the pipes, and all we could hear was folk hooching to the music. We all took it in turns to perform, and as usual sang a few choruses together.

When we had finished our performance all the lights came on, and there must have been at least three thousand people in front of us. What a shock. They wouldn't stop clapping.

While this was going on, I was speaking to Ian, when Cathie came over to me and said, 'Where is Mum?'

Well, we looked for her, but could we see her? No, we could not.

Just then we heard a commotion in the crowd. The body-guards jumped off the stage, and the next thing they were leading my mother back from the crowd. They told us to keep her backstage. Half of her tartan was torn off her. When she finished the performance she had jumped off the stage and got caught up in the crowd. They all wanted a bit of her tartan and had taken it whether she wanted to give it or not.

We flew home the next day, and I may say my mother was happy to get home. When I got back there was a letter waiting for me from Brittany. They wanted me to go the following week as one of seven participants to a festival in Rennes. I got ready and went off to France.

There were six of us in the end, as one of the participants couldn't make it. We arrived in Brittany and were shown to a beautiful hotel. We started the festival the next day, singing in big theatres. We were well looked after the whole time.

The day before we were due to come home, we were invited to get the freedom of the city of Mordelles. We arrived there, and proceedings started off with a champagne reception hosted by the Lord Mayor in his council offices. Then we all had to sign the golden book. After this they took us outside to the courtyard where there was a band waiting for us. We were piped through the city walking behind a group of bombards. If you have ever heard a bombard, you can imagine what six of them sound like – ear-piercing. So we got the freedom of the city. I always wanted to go back to see it, maybe someday I will.

I swore when I got home I would rest for a while. No such luck.

My mother wasn't too well when I got back, so I put her to bed for a few days until she was better.

A friend of mine came to see me, and told me there was a traveller family in a tent in a wee wood near Kirriemuir. The woman was due to have a baby, but the doctor or the nurse wouldn't go to see her. My friend asked if there was anything I could do. At this time I was working with the Secretary of State for Scotland on a project to help travellers.

I went to Kirriemuir. I had brought some things that would come in handy for a confinement, and also some food. When I approached the camp, a dog started barking at me, and a man appeared with a big cudgel in his hand. 'Who are you?' he said.

'It's alright, I'm a traveller tae,' I replied. 'I have come to help your wife. She is going to have a wain, isn't she?'

The man became less hostile then, and asked, 'How dae I ken you're a treveller?' So I started talking cant to him in my traveller way of speaking. He relaxed then.

I went in to see the woman in her tent. Her labour hadn't started yet, but she hadn't long to go. I made her comfortable and washed her face. She had a very bad black eye and a cut lip. She thanked me, and I said I would come back with habbin (food) for her.

When I came out of the tent, the man and two bairns were sitting round the fire looking very scruffy and depressed. The man's clothes were dirty and all ripped and torn, and the wains had a fear in their faces that alarmed me.

I looked at the man and said, 'Did you do that to her?'

'Me hit Jean? No way. Look at my face,' he said.

'I would if I could see it – there is so much dirt on your face I can't see anything.'

He went over to a basin, gave his face a bit of a clean, dried it and came and showed me his face. 'Oh my God, what happened to you?' His face looked as if it had been kicked three or four times with a hard boot.

'We were sitting round the fire last night,' he said, 'and the wains were sleeping in the tent, when we heard this noise coming towards us, and we knew it was drunk men. Nearer and nearer they came. There were three burly-looking men, like farm hands. Well, they got a hold o' my wife first, and gave her a few punches in the face. I stepped up to them and told them she was having a baby. Just like that, they turned tae me, knocked me down wi' a punch, and started kickin' into me. All the time they were saying, 'We hate you tinks, you are the scum of society. You all need to be herded onto an island away from decent society.' Then they left, laughing and talking about all the punches they got in.'

I looked at him in shocked disbelief, and I thought to myself, 'It's not the Middle Ages any longer, but travellers will always be persecuted.'

I left then, saying to the man, 'Look, your wife won't have her baby for a few hours yet, so I am going back to my house to get a few things I need. I will be back soon. Stay in your tent, and believe me they won't come back.'

I was away for about an hour and a half. My mother hadn't thrown away my dad's clothes, so I grabbed some for the man and took some of Roy's and Gregor's things for the boys. Some of my own and my mother's clothes would do for the woman. Our neighbour next door had a baby of six months old, and she gave me some peekie (baby) clothes for the new-born child.

I headed back to the camp. The man met me from the car and said his wife was having the baby. I rushed into the tent just as the baby came home. It was a wee plump girl, all wrinkly and beautiful.

I cleaned up the baby and the mother, made a fire in the woods to burn the things that needed to be burned, came back, washed my hands, and made them their dinner. I gave the man the clothes for him and the two boys, and told them to go down to the wee stream to wash and dress themselves. My goodness, did they look fresh and clean when they came back.

I fed them, and the boys were wolfing down the sloorich (a mixture of vegetables, tatties and meat) when I heard a whimper from the tent. It was the mother, who was asking for more sloorich. 'It's the best I have ever tasted,' she said.

'Well, I made plenty,' I said, 'it will last a few days.'

'Not if I get near the pot, it won't,' said the mother.

The husband came in laughing, and you could see he was proud of his wee daughter. I tidied up as best I could, and told them I had to go home. I got all the blessings of God from them, and wishes that I may never want. I kissed the kids and the woman. The man was standing kicking his feet, so I kissed him on the cheek as well.

Two days later I went back to the campsite, but they were gone.

About three months later, a traveller told me they called the wee girl Sheila, after me. I was delighted, and hoped I would see them again, but I never had the luck.

Some folk would say travellers were never treated like that, but I can guarantee you they were. I lost a lot of relations through the ignorance and ill-treatment of society long ago. We were hounded, persecuted and ridiculed. There was no reason for this. We might not have much education, but we have our own knowledge and common sense.

I was often consulted about people's problems. A friend of

mine came to see me one day, a traveller, and said she was being driven mad with her neighbours. She stayed in Hunter's Crescent in Perth. She asked me to come through and have a word with them. I looked at her and said, 'I'm not the police.'

'I ken that,' she said, 'but maybe they will pay attention to you.'

So next day I went to Perth, and got a different story. It was the woman who came to see me who was causing the trouble. She and her husband were having parties all the time, and her complaint was that their neighbours kept telling them to stop the noise. I confronted her about this, and she said, 'Why do they complain so much? We are only having a wee drink and an argument now and again, that's all.'

I looked at her and said, 'This has been a wasted journey for me. Sort it out yourselves.' Then I went home.

Another time I got a card from a traveller named Sooky. She lived in a wee cottage up Loch Tayside way, and she wanted my help. These travellers think I still work for them and am obliged to help them, like when I was on the Secretary of State's commission, but I don't mind – they are my people, after all, and I am proud of that. It was two days later when I headed up there to see what was wrong.

On my way there I met a man I know named Grizzly. He had a temper like a bear, but he was also a kind creature. 'Sheila, Sooky is waiting for you,' he said. 'I won't tell you what is wrong, she will do that herself.' He waved goodbye, and was gone.

Now, what I remembered about Sooky was that she was a very aggressive girl, but I thought maybe now that she was older she would have changed. When I got there, Sooky was at the door to meet me. 'Oh, Sheila, thank God you came! I am in deep trouble. I have to go to court in two days time, and I may get the quod [jail].'

I looked at her severely, and said, 'What have you done now? You and your temper!'

'No, no, Sheila, it wasn't my temper this time. It was for chorin' [stealing].'

151

'Chorin'! What did you chore, Sooky?'

'I went into the folks' hoose and stole habbin [food].'

'What did you do that for?'

'Sheila, me and the wains were hungry, and Willie is away workin' and won't be back till next week. Sheila, what am I going to do?'

'Where is your mother, or your sister Mina?' I asked.

'Mina is coming here the night, but I need you to speak for me at court. Will you, will you?' I heard the desperation in her voice, and I felt sorry for her.

'When is the court?' I asked.

'The day after tomorrow. You can sleep in the bed wi' wee Bengie if you like.'

'Who is Bengie?' I asked.

'My wee yaffin [dog].'

'Thanks, but no thanks. I'll sleep in my car.'

So we agreed. She made the dinner when Mina arrived at about five.

'What a silly thing to do, wasn't it, Sheila?' said Mina.

'Ah, but you must remember, Mina, must is a good master.'

Two days later we arrived at court. I spoke for Sooky, and said she had done it because of necessity, and we would pay for what she had taken to feed her kids. The woman who she stole off stood up when she heard all the facts, and said she wouldn't prosecute. The judge said that she couldn't go back on it now, once you are charged it sticks.

The judge looked at Sooky, and asked her if she would do it again. She said, 'Oh no, sir, once was enough for me. My man will be home tonight, and we will have money.'

Well, the judge thought for a while and then said, 'Case dismissed,' and hit his hammer on his desk. Sooky looked bewildered. Then it sank in. The biggest grin came over her face, and she hugged me.

That was a while ago, and I haven't heard from her since then.

22

Singing for the Pope

❧

One day in 1980 I got a phone call from a lady who lived in a castle ten miles away. She asked me to come to see her, as it was an important matter she wanted to discuss with me. I went out to the castle. The thing she wanted to ask me was, would I sing for Pope John Paul II on his visit to Scotland?

'Why me?' I asked.

'Well,' she said, 'the bishops in Glasgow wanted someone representing people who are underprivileged to sing to the Pope. So they decided to get someone from Europe. That's when I stepped in. I said, 'Why go to Europe? We have under-privileged people here in Scotland – the travelling people – and I know just the person to sing. Sheila Stewart.''

I was somewhat taken aback.

'Will you do it, Sheila?'

'I can't sing to the Pope,' I said. 'I am not a Catholic. I have no religion, really.'

'Sheila, the Pope doesn't mind,' she said. 'Will you do it? If so, I want you to come with me to meet the bishops in Glasgow, and we can sort everything out.'

So I agreed to at least go with her to see the bishops in Glasgow.

A few days later we went to Glasgow for the meeting. The bishops questioned me very carefully, I guess for the sake of security. The meeting lasted all morning. We had lunch and then went home. As we left, the bishops said they would come to the castle and see us in a week's time.

A week later I went to the castle, and while I was having a cup of tea their car pulled up. It was a scorching hot day, so we went into the front garden and had tea while we discussed the event. The bishops said I would have to make a short speech and then sing. The speech was to begin, 'I am a traveller, and I come from Scotland . . .' and so on.

They asked me if I would do it. I replied, 'Let me think it over, and I will let you know.' A week later I went out to the castle and said I would do it.

The lady told me what would happen on the day. The event was in Bellahouston Park. They were to build a small stage for me not far from the Pope's stage. I would have one microphone that would go to speakers in each of the enclosures of people that were there. Everyone was in enclosures that were marked with numbers matching their tickets, so that they would know where to go.

At last the big day arrived when I was to sing to the Pope. My small stage was on the side of a hill, overlooking the huge crowd of 385,000 people. On my right was the massive stage for the Pope, and on my left-hand side was another big stage where more performers were to appear. I was dressed from head to foot in my Royal Stewart tartan, and on my feet was a new pair of bright green shoes I had bought in honour of the Pope.

The Pope was arriving in a helicopter. There was complete silence as the crowd watched him land. To them it must have been an electrifying sight.

When the Pope sat down in his seat, only then did the crowd cheer. The sound was deafening. As it died away, a group from the stage on my left started to sing. They were fabulous.

Then it was my turn. I was introduced and all went silent again. I stepped up to the mike and started to speak. All I managed to get out were the words, 'I am a traveller . . .' and the whole of Bellahouston erupted. Things were getting thrown in the air – hats, bonnets and God knows what else – and they wouldn't stop applauding. The director came up to me with panic on his face. He shouted, 'Sing, just sing!' and I started to sing 'Go, Move, Shift' by Ewan McColl. All was silent; you could hear a pin drop.

Born in the middle of an afternoon
In a horsedrawn wagon on the old A5,
The big 12-wheeler shook my bed.
'You can't stop here,' the policeman said,

Chorus
'You'd better get born in someplace else,
So move along, get along,
Move along, get along,
Go! Move! Shift!'

Born in the tattie-lifting time,
In an old bow tent in a tattie field,
The farmer said, 'The work's all done,
It's time that you were moving on,'

Chorus

Born in a wagon on a building site,
Where the ground was rutted by the trailer's wheels,
The local people said to me,
'You'll lower the price of property,'

Chorus

Born at the back of a blackthorn hedge,
When the white hoarfrost lay all around,
No wise men came bearing gifts,
Instead the order came to shift,

Chorus

The winter sky was hung with stars,
And one shone brighter than the rest.
The wise men came so stern and strict
And brought the order to evict,

Chorus

Wagon, tent or trailer born,
Last week, last year or in far-off days,
Born here or a thousand miles away,
There's always men nearby who'll say,

'You'd better get born in someplace else,
So move along, get along,
Move along, get along,
Go! Move! Shift!'

When I finished, the crowd erupted again for about ten minutes.
I couldn't get off the stage quick enough, but the director kept
making me bow and bow. I had a crick in my back.

When I came off the stage, a few of the BBC staff and news
reporters came over to me and we sat and had lunch together.
It was a big relief to be finished. I wasn't tired, I just felt my
brain had stopped working, and the sense of relief left me
exhausted.

After the ceremony was all over, I was told to stand in a
special spot, as the Pope was coming round in his Popemobile.
I stood there for quite some time, and eventually the Popemobile stopped where I was standing. The Pope got out and
came over to me. He blessed me, put his hand on my shoulder
and said, in excellent English, 'I like the colour of your shoes!'
His smile was electric. He was the most pleasant dignitary I had
ever met in my life.

When I arrived back in Blairgowrie, people kept coming up
to me to touch my shoulder where the Pope had put his hand.
This went on for months. It was a nice thing for them to do, but
a terrible pressure on me after a while. However, I will never
forget the honour of singing a song for the Pope.

By this time I had taught Roy to sing unaccompanied, and he
had learned all my ballads. Roy had made his debut in London,
where we went on a short tour with my mother, young Ian,
Roy and me.

After that Roy and me were invited to go for a three weeks' tour to America to perform at festivals. Our first festival was an open-air one, and Roy and me were sharing a small stage with two Scottish-American singers, one of whom was a minister. We were all sitting round on chairs and each had to sing a song to start with. The minister was first. His voice was not bad, but the song he sang wasn't really traditional, in fact it was terrible. Then the other man sang, followed by me, and then it was Roy's turn. He sang 'Johnnie, My Man', and he sang it with the conyach in it (the feeling coming from the heart).

All three thousand people in the audience stood up cheering, and the rest of us never got singing any more; they would not let Roy off the stage. Mind you, he was only 11 years old. He sang one ballad after another.

That night they threw a party, with plenty to eat and drink, for everybody involved with the festival. However, Roy and me sneaked out to our bedrooms early, because they had started going round the room getting people to sing. We were tired, so we made our escape before it was our turn. They kept us out there for nearly three months. By the end of it we were so homesick we just wanted to go home.

It was a great experience for Roy. When he was a bit older his voice broke, and he won't sing now, or at least I haven't heard him. Here is the first song he sang. It was always a favourite with my uncle Donald and my uncle Andy. It never failed to bring a tear to their eyes.

Johnnie, My Man

Oh, Johnnie, my man, do you no' think o' rising,
The day's far and spent, and the nicht's coming on,
Yer siller's a' done and your stoup's teemed afore ye,
So rise up, my Johnnie, and come awa' hame.

'Noo, wha is't that I hear speaking sac kindly,
Tis surely the voice of my ain wifie Jean,

Come in–by my deary, and sit doon beside me,
Tis time enough yet to be gaan awa' hame.'

Oh, Johnnie, my man, wir wee bairnies are greeting,
There's nae meal in the barrel tae fill their wee wames,
While you sit here drinking, ye leave me lamenting,
So, rise up, my Johnnie, and come awa' hame.

Noo, Johnnie, he rose and he banged the door open,
Saying, 'Cursed be the tavern that e'er let me in,
And cursed be the whisky, that makes me sae thirsty,
So, rise up, my Jean and we'll haud awa' hame.'

Contented and cruse, he sits by his ain fireside,
And Jeannie a happier wife there is nane.
Nae mair tae the ale hoose at nicht does he wander,
But contented wi' Jean and his bairnies at hame.

23
Travellers' Culture

We just got back from America in time to get the last two weeks of the berry-picking, and to see some travellers. It was a great opportunity for my mother to see her friends again. We had a run up to see a camp where my mother's cousin always stayed. Her name was Margaret, but we called her Meg. She was sitting at the fire when we arrived, putting tea into her kettle.

'You are just in time,' she said, 'you must have smelled it!'

'Good,' said my mother. 'You cannae beat tea off an outside fire.'

Just then a wee boy came riding up on a bike and went right through the fire, knocking the kettle to one side all over Meg's legs. She fell back and started to scream.

The wee boy kept saying that he was sorry, but he had lost control of his bike. What he didn't say was that he had no brakes.

Everyone came running out of their tents when they heard her scream. I said I would take her down to the doctor.

'No. No doctor,' Meg said. 'Sandy,' she shouted, 'Come here!' and her son came over.

'Go to the field and get me a lot of dock leaves, big ones, and some water and earth. Now,' she said, turning to me, 'get my wee basin and clean it out and dry it, will you, Sheila?'

She was a strong woman, but there was severe pain in her face. When she saw me looking at her, she said, 'I can stand a lot of pain, I have had to all my life. I remember one year we were at the cutting of the corn, and I was only a slip o' a lassie then. I ran past my da just as he was coming down with the scythe, and it cut me on the ankles. You have no idea of the pain I have been through in my life.'

Sandy arrived with the dock leaves and his sister came with the water and the earth. Meg grabbed the basin I had cleaned and put in the earth, added the water and mixed them up like a poultice. Then she spread the mud on the dock leaves, took them and placed them on her legs. She tore a strip from her petticoat to tie the leaves on with and sank back, saying, 'Oh that's good and cool.' By this time my mother had the kettle boiling again and made us all tea.

After Meg had finished her tea, she fell sound asleep. My mother said to Jock, her man, 'We will be back to see if her legs are alright, Jock.'

'Fine, Belle, thanks. Goodnight, Sheila,' he said to me.

'I will be back tae, Jock. Goodnight,' I said.

Two days later we went back up to the camp to see how Meg was. She was sitting near the fire, but her legs weren't covered.

'Come in, come in, Belle and Sheila, and sit doon. The tea is ready this time. I feel a lot better the day.'

She stood up with no bother and lifted up her skirt to show us her legs. We looked at where the burns had been, and there was only a wee patch of red on each leg. There wasn't a scab in sight; they were as clean as a whistle.

'The only thing I can't dae is to sit too close to the fire just now, but when they are completely healed they will be fine.'

Travelling folk have many cures of their own. Long ago we didn't run to the doctor every time we felt ill. We tried to cure ourselves in those days, but now even travellers don't bother with the old cures any more.

There are one or two aspects of our culture I would like to point out to readers.

We travelling people have our own ways about things. Our dishes, for example. We would never wash our dishes in a sink. We had a special basin for them, and it was not used for anything else in the family. Dish towels were boiled in a pot on the fire, rinsed in the clean dish basin, and hung out separately from other clothes. My mother would drape paper over the rope before she would hang dish-towels up, because clothes had hung on the rope the day before.

In a house we would never put a cup on the floor. To us that was dirty. If people who visited us did it, for example the collectors who came to us long ago, they were told in no uncertain terms not to put them there.

Other children at school used to call me a dirty traveller (or dirty tinker in my younger days). However we have a cleanliness of our own that people don't see. I myself, if a spoon fell into my sink, would take it and bend it and throw it away. No matter how much you clean a sink, bleach it or disinfect it, nothing would make me wash my dishes in a sink.

All travellers held these beliefs. Another one was to do with horses. My uncle Donald used to say the cleanest animal alive was a horse. It even strains water through its teeth. We were happy to let horses drink out of our clean bucket.

Travellers always said that there is only one animal that can see the wind, and that is a pig. True or not, who knows?

That reminds me of another wee story my uncle Donald told me. He said he was coming home one day back to his tent after a few drams. There was a terrible wind blowing. He sat down to light his pipe. At first he could not get it lit with the match, but he finally got it going, and relaxed to have a puff. All of a sudden, the wind that was blowing changed and he could see it. It was blowing in gusts of fire, like the fiery flames of hell. The wind was still cold but he could see the flames dancing around his body. He sat dumbstruck, paralysed and terrified. The fiery wind lasted for about five minutes, then it disappeared as quickly as it had come. Uncle Donald swore he had seen the wind in its true form that day.

One day we heard there had been a big, big fight at the Ponfaulds, where the travellers stayed during the berry-picking. There were some people hurt, but being travellers they wouldn't go to a doctor. I told my mother I would go out and see what was going on.

'No, no, Sheila, don't go,' she said.

'They won't touch me, mother, don't be silly.'

So I went out there. Some of the caravans were wrecked, after travellers had driven their big lorries into them. There was a gathering of travellers at one part of the green, and I drove up to ask them what had happened.

'What went on here last night?' I said.

'Oh my God, Sheila, it all started off over a couple of the young ones driving a big lorry through the green and nearly ploughing into two bairns. Showing off they were. The father of one of the wee bairns came out of his caravan and went mad, and kicked the boys' arses a few times. Which I think was quite right, but, Sheila, its not what it used to be – if a bairn did wrong, travellers were allowed to chastise them, and they also got a smack from the parents as well, but no' now. Then all hell broke loose! They started fighting each other and wrecking everyone's caravans and lorries. The farmer sent for the police, but when they came everything had quietened down. They had a look and said to the farmer, 'It's only a tinkers' squabble', and drove off again.'

'Is anyone badly hurt?' I asked.

'Mo has a sore leg, and Henny has a burst nose and sore ribs, that's all I know about.'

'God bless my soul, how can they no' behave themselves?' I said.

'That's easy, Sheila: peeve [drink].'

I agreed with her wholeheartedly. There was nothing I could do, so I went home, and told my mother all that had happened.

The next day Hamish Henderson came to see us with an American collector. He asked us if we would do a concert at the Edinburgh Festival Fringe in a week's time, and we agreed. Cathie, me and my mother went to the concert. It was a good night with a lot of folk-song collectors there. We stayed the night with Ella Ward, a great friend of ours. As usual we never got paid for the concert, the story of our life. But we didn't care – Hamish was our friend, so we didn't say anything.

We read in the paper that a good friend of my parents had died, and we decided to go to the funeral in Dundee. 'We will go, Sheila,' said my mother, 'but we won't stay long, because they are awfy peevers [drinkers].'

It was the coldest funeral I was ever at – I don't mean the weather, but the atmosphere. It was gloomy and terrible. The son hadn't even arrived when it was time for the service, which was held at the graveside. He finally arrived half-drunk. There was no minister there, just a travelling man to take the service. He made an announcement that he could not get a minister to conduct the ceremony because he would not come to a traveller's funeral. 'So I am doing it,' he said, and he started.

He was halfway through the service when the son chimed in, he put his hand in the air and said, 'Stop, I want a sloosh [pee].' He went over to a tombstone, turned his back and relieved himself. Then he came back and said, 'Carry on now.' My mother and me were mortified.

At the end of the funeral we were invited to go for a drink in a pub. 'No thanks,' my mother whispered to me.

We were leaving the churchyard when a thin woman came up to my mother. 'Belle, is that you?'

I don't think her face had been washed for about a month, and it had dried blood on it. Her knuckles also were covered in blood. My mother answered, 'Is that you, Bi?'

'Aye, faith, it's me, alright.'

My mother hugged her and said, 'Bi, this is my lassie, Sheila.'

She put out her hand to me and I shook it. She apologised for the mess she was in. My mother said to her, 'Whatever happened to you?'

She replied, 'It was him last night,' meaning her man. 'I got him lifted, though. That is the last time he will put his hands on me, ever.' She was already moving away. 'Goodbye, Belle,' she said, 'Keep well, old friend.' Off she went, never looking back.

When we got into the car, my mother turned to me and said, 'Don't start the car just now, Sheila. I want to tell you about Bi. She was my friend since I was wee. She is the nicest person you will ever meet. She has respect for others, but not for herself. She is couthy, and used to be a beautiful young girl, not that you can see it now. That man was the ruin of her. She gets beaten up all the time. I hope this time he's gone for good. She will always be my friend. Never judge by what a person looks like, Sheila, she has a soul.'

Me and my mother went for our weekly shopping down to the supermarket for the first time. This was the new way to shop. It was a shock for us, being travellers, to be allowed to pick up food for ourselves. We found it strange, and we were afraid that people would think we were stealing. At first we were paranoid, thinking everybody was watching us. It took a long time for me to feel comfortable with this way of shopping, but I finally got used to it. It took my mother longer, so I got the groceries and my mother just walked beside me.

That day we were standing in a queue at the check-out, when we heard a woman whisper to her friend, 'That's Belle Stewart, she got the BEM. How can they give a tink an honour like that?'

My mother walked up to her and said, 'I didn't get it for gossiping, anyway, and if you don't shut your mouth I will shut it for you, you old bat!'

The teller at the check-out laughed, and said, 'Good for you, Belle.' The woman and her friend were so ashamed they left their messages in the trolley, and virtually ran out of the shop.

We could only laugh at this silly episode. The check-out girl said, 'Never mind them, they are only fools.'

My mother looked at her and said, in a cheery voice, 'My dear, if we were all sensible there would be nae fools.'

We laughed again. 'I must remember that, Belle,' said the check-out girl, 'it's a great saying.'

24
Passing on the Tradition

I was out visiting a cousin one day. When I came back, my
mother was sitting on the couch and said to me, 'Sheila, I have
written a poem while you were away. It's about Blair. Sit doon
and I will read it to you.' So I sat down, and listened.

'It's called 'Oor Toon',' she said.

> Blairgowrie is a bonny place,
> It's there I like tae bide,
> Although I've been in many lands,
> And across the ocean wide.
>
> But there's something in that wee toon,
> That fills my hert wi'glee,
> And there's nae place, on a' the earth,
> That I would rather be.
>
> The folk are nice and kindly,
> And I like them ane an a',
> And many a time I've thocht o' them,
> When I am far awa'.
>
> There's been many changes in the toon,
> Since I cam' here a bairn,
> But of course ye ken the sayin's true,
> Ye have to live and learn.
>
> But ye ken I'm o' a different class,
> And I'm no' the same as you,

But it takes all kinds to make a world,
Again that sayin's true.

For I've mixed wi' lords and ladies,
And folk o' high degree,
I've been in many foreign lands,
Some bonny sichts tae see.

But tae tell the truth sincerely,
And I think it's only fair,
The place that I like best o' a'
Is our ain wee toon o' Blair.

Although we were persecuted in Blair, and got beaten up for being travellers, my mother loved Blairgowrie, and I would like the people of Blair to remember that.

My mother and me were asked to go to the USA again, and this time it was for a week's teaching ballads and lecturing on the travelling oral culture in Elkins, West Virginia. The Americans love Scottish and Irish oral tradition, and we got a good welcome. We arrived on the Friday and had time to settle in, because we didn't start teaching till Monday. So we chilled out for a couple of days, and went to the ceilidhs at night.

One night we were sitting in the big concert hall, listening to the music, and at half time I went out for a smoke. I was standing there when two men came up to me. In an American drawl, one said to me, 'Are you Sheila Stewart, from Scotland?'

'Yes, I am,' I said.

'Could you come with us for a few minutes?' the man asked.

I followed them over to a truck parked in the car park. One of the men took out a clay jug like you would see in the films, a big jar that hillbillies would have. He poured some liquid out of the jug into a plastic cup.

'We are neighbours,' he said. 'I make whisky, and my neighbour makes whisky, and we have come to you to tell us which one is the best.'

I couldn't believe my ears, but I was pleased they had asked me for my opinion. I didn't know anything about whisky, but I could not let Scotland down

'Taste it,' he said.

It was clear liquid, like water, the same colour as Irish poteen. I took a sip and swirled it round my mouth. It nearly took the skin off my tongue. I swallowed it, and said to him in a dignified manner, pretending I was an authority on whisky, 'My, my, that was powerful,' and nodding my head. A grin came over his face.

I looked sternly at him and said, 'You have done the wrong thing there, because you should never drink good whisky out of a plastic cup, it's a hanging offence.'

'Is it?' he said.

'Yes,' I replied, 'and it never tastes as good, either.'

The other man said to me, 'It's my turn now,' and he poured some of his own whisky into the same cup. I sipped it again and swirled it round, and if I hadn't had my tonsils out when I was young, I swear they would have been pickled.

'Now, which one is the best?' they asked, and waited on tenterhooks for my answer.

'Your one was a bit earthy,' I said to the first man, 'but it had a touch of sweetness in it, with vigorous power. A great whisky.' He was grinning from ear to ear.

Now it was the second man's turn. What could I say about his whisky? Oh, God help me, I thought. 'Your one was peaty, full-bodied and with a small hint of honey in it,' I said.

God must have helped me out, because the man said, 'How did you know I put a touch of honey in it?'

Maybe a bit too cocky by now, I looked at him and said, 'I am Scottish, you know!'

They both smiled at me, shook my hand and said, 'It's good meeting a professional in liquor.' They gave me the plastic tumbler filled with whisky, and went away two contented men. I didn't know whisky from lemonade, but they were happy.

I got back into the concert with the cup in my hand and sat down beside my mother. 'Ah, great,' she said, 'water!' and before I could stop her she had taken a big gulp of the whisky. She spluttered it out all over the man sitting in front of her, and headed for the door like a scalded cat. I got to the door behind her and collapsed in hysterical laughter. That night I can safely say she had a good sleep.

I was excited about starting the class on the Monday. My mother and I were separated – she had her classroom, and I had mine, which I thought was great. I had about 20 pupils, both men and women.

One man turned up with rather a cocky attitude. He was dressed in full Highland dress. 'What have I got here?' I wondered.

I introduced myself, and told the class I needed to hear what they could do before I could tell what they needed from me. I went along the line asking their names and what they did, till I came to the man in the kilt. He said, 'My name is Gary Morrison. I am a Scottish singer.' I looked at him and said, 'Wonderful.'

I went back over the line again and they all sang for me. There were some great voices among them. Now I came to Gary. He had a friend sitting beside him, who stood up and went to the piano. I was gobsmacked.

The piano started up and Gary announced what song he was singing. He sang with severe elocution. His mouth opened so wide sometimes you could have put a melon in sideways. His lips were all over the place. He sang, 'It's afar Cuillins are putting love on me, I step aye wi' my cromach to the road.'

When he finished I applauded him and smiled. 'What am I going to do with him,' I was thinking to myself. Then it struck me – here was a great challenge for me, to make a Scottish singer into a traditional folk-singer. Oh, my, my, I said to myself. Short, sharp treatment required, I think. That's what I will do with our Gary.

At the end of the session, I took him aside and said, 'Gary, don't come with the kilt tomorrow, and get rid of your pianist as well.'

'Alright, Sheila, I will, but I can't sing without backing music,' he replied.

I looked at him and said, 'That's what you think.'

With having to work with the other pupils, I felt that had been a day wasted for Gary. That night at dinner I said to him, 'I want to see you on your own tonight. We have a lot of work to do.' He said that would be fine.

So after dinner we met in a room connected to the dormitory where I was sleeping. First I had to get him to relax, both in his inner tension and his speech.

'Who told you to sing like that, Gary?' I asked.

'My music teacher. She gave me elocution lessons and told me how to dress.'

I said to him, 'Well, Gary, I am going to strip you of all you have been taught. Tell me if this is alright, or do you want to stay as you are? It is your choice.'

'I want to be the same as you, Sheila. I want to get into folk music. I didn't know this other type of Scottish singing, traditional oral ballads, existed. That's what I want to do.'

'Well, we have very hard work ahead of us, Gary. Are you ready?'

'Yes, I'm ready, Sheila.'

Getting him to relax was not easy, because he had that inbuilt tension within him. But I gave it a good try. The next night, though Gary didn't usually drink, I bought a bottle of wine. I rubbed my hands together and said to myself, this will work. I fed him the wine, not too much, just enough to make him relax and shake off the tension. I made him slouch in his chair and stop being stiff, and by God, the wine did it. I was so pleased.

Word went round the whole campus, and people were coming up to me, saying, 'Sheila, you will never do anything with him.' This made me more determined to carry on.

Every lunchtime and evening we worked at Gary's singing and the other pupils didn't know what we were doing. On the

Friday, we had to present our pupils and what they had learned. I wanted Gary's singing to be a surprise, and I told him put the kilt back on to keep our secret. 'On Friday, Gary,' I said to him, 'I am putting you on last.'

Friday arrived, and I was shaking with nerves and fear. I kept whispering to myself, 'Please, please, Gary, don't let me down.'

The presentation was held in a concert hall with a big audience of students, staff and families. All the head people running the school were there to see what I had done with my pupils. We started the presentation, and each of the pupils did their bit. I had taught them ballads to sing as well, and they performed them beautifully. I was searching the audience for Garry and couldn't see him. When it came to his turn, I was desperate. 'He is not here,' I thought.

I announced him anyway. A few moments passed, then there was a movement at the back of the hall and Gary walked up to the stage. He was unrecognisable. He had jeans on with a hole in the knee and his hair was tousled. He was tidy but folky, and, my goodness, he looked the part.

He opened his mouth and started singing in such a relaxed way. I was more tense than he was. His performance was terrific. Remember, he had no musical backing. Everyone in the hall gave him a standing ovation. What a night that was.

The head of the school, Margo, asked me to come and teach the course again next year, I said, 'Wait till I get my breath back!'

Outside our dormitory there was a big party and a lot of folk there. They had an enormous pot full to the brim with corn on the cob. We had a good feed, and of course there was drink as well. Gary came up to me and said, 'Sheila, I can never thank you enough. You have made a different man of me. What is my girlfriend going to say when I go back home? She is a bit of a snob, and thinks that the way I used to sing was the right way. Our marriage will be off!' He was giggling a lot, and I noticed he had a glass of wine in his hand. That set me off laughing as well.

That wasn't the last I heard about Gary. A few years later, my son Ian went to a show in Alabama in the States to sell bagpipes that he had made and other touristy things. He was standing at his stall surrounded by customers. A man nearby was looking at him strangely, and obviously listening to the way Ian was speaking. When the crowd thinned out, he came over. 'Sorry if I was staring at you,' he said, 'but the way you talk sparked something off in my mind. Have you come straight over from Scotland to sell your wares?'

'Yes, I have,' said Ian. 'Why do you ask?'

'There's something, but there couldn't possibly be a connection,' the man replied.

'Tell me what it is,' said Ian.

'You wouldn't know a woman called Sheila Stewart, would you?' asked the man.

Ian looked at him, astonished, and said, 'That's my mother!'

Ian said the look on his face was one of shock, then happiness. He cuddled Ian, saying 'Oh my God, oh my God! My name is Gary. Your mother taught me how to sing!'

When he had calmed down, he said, 'That woman completely changed my life forever. Tell her I married my girlfriend, and she accepted the new me. Give her a hug from me.'

I was delighted to be told Ian had come across Gary, it made my teaching of him complete. I was so relieved to hear that he was happy.

25
A Couple of Stories

When we arrived home from America, my sister Rena was very ill. She had cancer of the pancreas, and was in Edinburgh Royal Infirmary. We knew she was suffering from this before we went, but we didn't realise how unwell she was.

A week later she died. My lovely wee sister had gone. She was a jewel of a person, and to me she will always be my girl.

The funeral was a nightmare for me, the thought that I would never see her again was unbearable. I know she is in no pain now, but that didn't help my grief at the time. I miss her so much.

Rena was very well educated, and had become the registrar in Blairgowrie. Her daughter is a top-notch lawyer with a big firm in London, and her son also stays in England. They are two great kids, and I am very proud of them.

In August about a year afterwards, I was coming out of the house one day when I met a woman carrying a small boy, about three years old, who was crying his eyes out. I had seen the woman before. She was a traveller called Maisie and was in Blairgowrie for the berry-picking.

She said the wee boy had been stung by a wasp when he was having a pee, and the sting was right on the point of his pintle. I took her into the house. She took his trousers off, and his wee pintle was swollen like a small balloon. When my mother saw it she said she felt the pain as well as the boy.

First making sure the sting was not in the boy, my mother went away and got white vinegar and poured it over the boy's pintle. The wee boy screamed his head off.

I started the car and took them to the doctor. The doctor said my mother had done the right thing, but that the boy must have had a lot of pain when the vinegar went on the sting. 'He will be fine now, and the vinegar will take down the swelling. It will be better in the morning.'

I asked my mother how she knew to put vinegar on it, and who had told her what to do.

'Nobody told me, it was all I had in the kitchen at the time,' she replied. She and her old-fashioned doctoring! But it worked, even without her knowing it would. Me being me, I didn't tell her she had done the right thing.

The next evening we took a walk to where the travellers' camp was. The woman and her son had moved out that morning, but the wee boy was fine.

There were lots of things about health that we travellers shared long ago. We only trusted each other. The lack of trust of other people was because we never mixed with country hantle (non-travellers), and they didn't bother to mix with us.

Here is a story about travellers that my father told me long ago.

The Voice at the Door

This is a story about a travelling man and woman, who were tramping the road away up in the north of Scotland. They were walking up through a glen, and the rain was coming down in torrents. They had no place to go, no caravan and no tent, they had nothing. The woman was carrying a small child about six weeks old.

They were walking up this glen, and up this glen, and the man turned to his wife, and said, 'We will have to get some kind of shelter, or that bairn's going to die.'

He looked up and saw a dim light in front of them. 'Look,' he said to his wife, 'see that light over there, it must be a house.'

'You're right,' she said, 'it is a house.'

They went up to the house and rapped on the door. The door opened and a man came out. 'Well,' he said, 'what do you want?'

The travelling man asked him if this was a farm, and was he the farmer.

'Yes, I am the farmer.'

'Sorry to bother you, sir, but could you please let us into one of your barns? We are frozen to the skin, and so is our child.'

'Oh my goodness,' said the farmer. 'You had better come inside, and bring in your wife and child in too.'

So they went into the house, and the farmer's wife gave them something to eat. When they had finished, the farmer said to them, 'I've a little cotter house up on the side of the hill. I will go up with you and I'll take the lantern with me. There's a bed and some blankets in there. You can stay in there tonight, and we will see what can be done in the morning.'

'Alright,' said the travelling man, 'and God bless you, sir, for your kindness.'

So the farmer took them up to the wee house and opened the door. 'There are plenty of sticks in the shed,' he said, 'so you can make a fire, and I'll see you in the morning.'

After the farmer had left them, they kindled a big fire and made the bed.

Next morning, the man got up and said, 'I must go down now and see the farmer.'

Off he went in the pouring rain, as it hadn't cleared up at all during the night. He got to the farmhouse and knocked on the door, and the farmer opened it.

'Good morning, farmer,' said the travelling man. 'I would like to ask you if you have any work I can do. We can't sit in the cottage without doing work for you.'

'You can't work in this kind of weather,' said the farmer. 'I have a field of neeps in the field down there that are needing shawing [harvested and trimmed]. But the weather would kill you, man.'

'It'll no' kill me to go down there and shaw a couple of rows o' neeps for you,' said the travelling man.

So the farmer just shook his head and gave him a huke [cutter used to trim the turnips], and he went away down to the field.

He shawed away at the neeps, and he shawed right up until five o'clock that night. He stopped then and went away back up to the wee house.

The farmer came up with some food for them, and he said, 'You shouldn't have gone out, man, it was too wet. You're soakin' right through.'

'Ah,' said the travelling man, 'I'll be fine, I'm alright.'

But during the middle of the night the travelling man became very ill. He turned to his wife and said, 'I'm not well at all, wife. I don't know what's wrong with me.'

'I told you about going out in that weather, but no, you wouldn't pay attention to me.'

As the night went on he got a lot worse, so his wife decided she would go down to the farmer to see what he thought they should do. Away down to the farmhouse she went and rapped on the door.

The farmer came out and said, 'What's wrong now?'

She replied, 'My man's very ill, sir. He can hardly speak, and he is getting worse every minute.'

'My goodness, I told him this morning it was too wet to go and work.'

'Yes,' she said, 'and I told him tae, but he wouldn't pay any attention.'

'I'll put my coat on and I will be with you in a minute,' said the farmer.

So he got his coat and boots on. He followed the traveller's wife up to the cottage, and when they got there he was unconscious.

'My goodness,' said the farmer, 'he is really ill. I will get the trap, and go for the doctor.'

He yoked up the pony to the trap, and went down to the village to get the doctor. The doctor came back up with the farmer and examined the traveller. 'This man's got pneumonia,' he said, 'and it is a very bad attack of it, I may say.'

He asked the woman if she had anything to make a poultice.

'I have nothing but oatmeal,' she replied.

'Well, make one with oatmeal and put it on him, and I'll be back in the morning.'

So the woman made a poultice with oatmeal and put it on him. But, oh, he got worse and worse, and he passed away during the night.

The woman went down again to the farmer to tell him her man was dead.

'My goodness gracious,' he said, 'that's terrible.'

The farmer came up with her to the cottage and said to her, 'Just you leave everything to me, I'll see that he gets buried alright.'

The undertaker arrived the next morning, stretched him out and put him in his coffin.

The farmer said to the woman, 'Will you be alright tonight, my dear? Are you frightened staying here with him on your own?'

'Not me,' said the woman. 'After all, he is my man. There is nothing going to harm me. I know he is dead, but he won't harm me.'

'No,' said the farmer, 'I don't expect he will.' He left her and went home.

About eleven o'clock that night, the woman went to her bed. She was lying there thinking, looking up at the ceiling, when she heard *scrape, scrape*, at the door of her room.

'My God,' she thought, 'what's that? It sounds like a dog scraping at the door.'

But the next thing she heard was a voice saying, 'Let me in, let me in.'

'Oh my God,' she thought to herself, and said out loud, 'Who's there?'

'I am your husband, let me in.'

'Oh no,' she said, 'my husband is dead through in the room.'

'No, no,' said the voice. 'It's me. Let me in, let me in.'

She was so frightened, she wouldn't open the door of her room, and the voice and the scraping kept going on like that the whole night.

The next morning she couldn't get out of bed. After a while, the farmer came up to the cottage. 'Are you up yet?' he asked.

She answered him, saying, 'Come on in, come on in. There's something happened last night that I cannae tell you yet. So come on in, come on in to the kitchen.'

So the farmer opened the door, and when he looked in, he saw the man out of his coffin, lying stone dead on the floor.

Well, the man was buried that day. The woman got a job on the farm, and her wee boy grew up there. When he was about 15, she left and went away to London. The woman stayed in London till she died, and that's the end of my story (as my father always said at the end of all his stories).

26
A Grand Old Lady

My brother Andy was next of my family to die. He had the same illness as my father, pernicious anaemia. He died at home. What a blow that was to the family. For me that was a brother and a sister I had lost.

Andy was devoted to his wife and kids. He had twin boys – lovely boys, and identical twins. His death was a great loss to them, and to his four daughters and wife. She was a devoted wife and a great sister-in-law. She died a few years later from cancer. She never was the same after Andy died.

His oldest daughter went abroad on holiday with her husband. She took ill with a brain haemorrhage and died over there. She was the nicest woman you could ever meet, and left a boy and girl.

Not long ago Andy's youngest daughter was killed in a car crash. She left three daughters. There are now only two girls and the boys left. We are all very close.

I also lost a granddaughter, Christina Grace, she died at birth. That, I think, was the hardest death to get over for me and my kids. She is buried with her grandfather Ian in Blairgowrie.

Next to die in the family was my oldest brother, John. His illness was the opposite of Andy's and my father's – he made too much blood, and had to go into hospital and get blood taken off him. I lost my father to blood problems, then Andy and now John. John had a son and a daughter. He owned a caravan site, and he and his son were berry-farmers. His daughter has a motel and is doing well, but life will never be the same for them, any more than it is for me.

I had one sister left, and that was Cathie, but I felt that my family were slowly disappearing around me.

My mother was getting a bit old now, and forgetful. She took Alzheimer's. I looked after her for eight years after that. Sometimes it was hard to watch your mother deteriorating in front of your eyes and becoming senile. During these years I never went singing or performing, I just looked after her full-time.

I may say she was funny at times. My mother had always had a great sense of humour, but her jokes were now becoming reality to her. At one point I asked her about my father, 'Your husband Alex, mother,' I said.

'Husband? I was never married, may God forgive you,' she replied, and with the next breath, 'Your father was a great man, Sheila. I was happy towards the end of his life.'

My mother was going to leave her house in Yeaman Street, Rattray, to Rena. After Rena's death, her husband and kids wanted the house, so I had to get another place for us both. I got a flat in Blairgowrie above a bookie's shop. The only problem was that it was on the first floor, and my mother couldn't manage the stairs. The man who owned it also owned a florist's shop on the ground floor. He was the best landlord I ever had. I have known him all my life, he is a gem, and so is his wife. Thank you, Lawrence Hill, and to your wife, for all your kindness to me and my mother.

The doctors in Blair, Dr McKay and Dr Sims, were wonderful as well. I am grateful to them too for being so good.

We had a lot of visitors, especially travellers, coming to see my mother. She didn't know who half of them were, but she pretended she did. She was a fly old woman, but courteous to everyone.

Cathie came up to see us one day and said to me, 'Sheila, I have finally learned a story. I remembered it last night. My granny told me it many years ago.'

She was so excited about remembering a story. For years we had been trying to get Cathie interested in telling stories, but she could never be bothered. I was excited as well. Cathie was the only one left in the family who could go on the stage with me. My mother was no longer able to.

'Sheila, please, please, let me tell it to you.'

'Maybe I know it already,' I said.

'No, you don't,' she said, with a broad smile on her face and a touch of sarcasm in her voice.

My mother was nodding off to sleep on her chair as Cathie sat down on the couch, and began.

The Vinegar Bottle

(There's a moral to this story, and it's about greed.)

Once upon a time there was an old man and an old woman, and they lived in a vinegar bottle. They had no house, in fact they had no possessions at all. The old man never used to go outside at all. He was always sitting about on his chair, and his wife was really fed up with him.

One day she was trying to sweep the floor, but he was getting in the way.

'Oh, I am fed up with this vinegar bottle!' she said. 'There is no room in it at all, and you're no help, old man. Can you no' go for a walk till I clean up?'

So he got up, lifted his pipe and paper, and went out. He was saying to himself, 'I am fed up with that woman, all she does is complain and moan all day and every day. She wants a house. She's lucky she is getting fed, never mind a house.'

He walked down to a wee stream near the vinegar bottle and sat down on a stone. He was grumbling out loud to himself about his wife, when he heard a rustle in the bushes and a wee man popped up. 'Hello there, John. What's the matter with you?'

'Oh, it's that wife of mine. She does nothing all day but moan. I am fed up with her.'

'Is that all?' said the wee man. 'Away you go home now, and everything will be fine.'

So John went home, and as he was coming to where the vinegar bottle should be, there was a big mansion house in its place. His wife came running out of the house, screaming her head off.

'John, you have done it, you have given me my house!'

She dragged him inside, and they explored the house together.

Time wore on again, and a few weeks passed, then she started her grumbling again. She went on and on about the house being too big for her to clean all by herself. Now she wanted staff to run the house and help clean it, lots of servants and a butler.

John got fed up with her grumbling again. He lifted his pipe and paper, walked down to the wee stream and sat down on the same stone. He kept repeating out loud, 'That silly woman is going to drive me mad!'

Up pops the wee man again. 'Well, John, what's wrong this time?' So John told him about her complaining because she wanted cleaners, maids, a cook and a butler.

'You go home, John,' said the wee man, 'and everything will be fine.'

Off John went back up to the house, and standing at the front door was a butler. 'Madam is in the parlour, Sir,' said the butler.

In went John to find a very happy wife, delighted that she now had all the servants she had wanted to help run the house.

All was fine for a few weeks, and then she started grumbling again.

'What's wrong with you now, woman?' said her husband.

'Well, John, what good is all this to us without money? I need jewellery, carriages, fine clothes and furs to keep up with our new status. Now go back again and ask the wee man to give us money.'

'Never,' said John. 'I will not go and ask him for anything else, no matter what you say or do.'

But his wife kept screaming at him about going to see the wee man again.

So off he went, and when the wee man asked him again what was wrong, John told him everything his wife wanted.

'Go back, John,' said the wee man, 'and all will be fine.'

John headed back up the path to go home, and when he got there the big mansion was gone, and his wife was back into the vinegar bottle.

'Now, that's what you get for being too greedy,' said Cathie.

I stared at her and said, 'But Cathie, you know that I know that story!'

'Ah, but you are missing the point. I told it, not you. It's my first story. I said to you I couldn't tell a story, but I have proved myself wrong!'

I burst out laughing, and I was laughing so hard, it woke my mother up. Cathie was laughing as well, though at what, she didn't know.

'What's all the laughing about, you lassies?' said my mother. We didn't answer.

'I know youse were laughing at me,' she said.

We didn't answer her, so she was none the wiser.

As I mentioned before, the stairs were a great problem for my mother. One day a woman from the council came to see me, and she told us we had got a council house in a newly built scheme in Old Rattray.

I was so happy I cried, because the house had a big garden at the back, and I thought my mother would be so happy to be able to sit out in the sun. How wrong I was!

I put her into a home for respite for a week, so that I could get us moved into the house. She escaped and was heading for Blair carrying a carrier bag of her things, and when she got to the Boat Brae she tripped and fell. She hurt herself and blacked her eye. They kept a closer watch on her after that, till I came to take her out.

Two days afterwards we were settled into our new house. It was a fine day, so my Heather said to me, 'Mum, you should put Ma [that's what everybody called my mother] outside for a wee while today, she would love that. I will help you get her ready.'

So we put her coat on and wrapped her up in her cosy blanket, took out her chair and got her to sit in it. From the minute she sat down she started grumbling about it. 'What am I doing here, Sheila?' she asked.

'You are getting some fresh air, Mother.'

She answered, 'I'm bad aboot fresh air. I have had all the fresh air I want over the years. Do you know this song, 'Take me in now, I'm frozen'?'

That was my mother. She didn't want anything to do with outside, she felt safer indoors. I never attempted to take her out again, except for runs in the car, and she wasn't too keen on that, either.

One day she was sitting counting her fingers, and she was awful quiet. I pulled a chair up beside her, and said to her, 'Mother, I am going to sing to you.'

'Oh, great,' she replied.

I said to her, 'Do you know this song, Mother?' and I sang two verses of 'The Berryfields o' Blair'. Her response was, 'Well, I have heard that before, but never learned it.'

I burst out laughing. 'Mother, you wrote that song.'

'Well, if I did, I have forgotten the words. But I don't need the words when you can sing them to me.'

She had logic in her, I thought. Why bark when you have a dog. I laughed again.

Her 90th birthday came that year, and I had a party for her up at the Old Mill. All the folk-singers came, even those from London. Hamish Henderson was there, as was Tim Neat, all friends from the folk scene. My family cooked all the food for the party.

It was a great day. Everyone enjoyed themselves, and my mother loved it, as far as I could tell. She had a huge birthday cake and also got a lot of presents. All her friends sang to her and played instruments. She couldn't sing herself, because by this time she couldn't hold a tune or remember the words. The party was even filmed and shown on television. All in all, it was a great success.

After about an hour, she shouted my son Ian over and whispered to him, 'Can I go hame now, son? I'm tired.' So me and Ian took her home. I put her to bed and she passed out into a good sleep until morning.

She slept late the next day, and when she woke up and was having her breakfast, I asked her if she had enjoyed her party.

'Party? What party? I haven't been to a party in years,' she said.

Her memory was getting worse, but she knew every one of the family. She never forgot any of us.

A few months afterwards she was getting out of bed, stubbed her toe on her Zimmer and cut it. I put her back to bed. My mother was diabetic, and I was frightened that once she had cut her big toe it would become infected. Luckily, the nurse was due to come that day.

When the nurse looked at the cut she just told me to keep it clean and bandaged, which I did. My mother stayed in bed for a week. I tried to get her up one day, but her toe was too sore to stand on, so I left her in bed. I dressed the wound twice a day, and I asked her if it was sore. 'No,' she said, 'only when I stand up.'

A few days later I sent for the doctor. He had a look at her foot and said she needed morphine. I wouldn't be able to give it to her, so she would have to go into the cottage hospital for it to be administered.

Next day I got her ready, and I took her into hospital. She lasted about four days, and she passed away in her sleep. Trust my mother, she was sitting on the commode at the time.

It was a terrible time for the family. The woman I had looked up to all my life was gone. Who was going to tell me what to do now? Really, I was on my own. I had my kids, but my mother and father, the heads of our family, were no longer with us. My mother was a grand old lady, and I miss her so much.

Her funeral was a very large one and many people came. She is buried in Alyth. I held a memorial concert for her and my father, and raised enough money to buy them a headstone, with their photos on it.

27
Kidnapped

My daughter Heather came to me one day a few weeks after the funeral and said, 'Mum, what are you going to do now? Are you going to be a bingo granny, and bake for the grandchildren, or what?'

I said, 'What do you think I should do?'

'Go out singing again, of course, what else?'

'But I have been off it for years. Maybe folk have forgotten me,' I replied.

'Are you kidding? The Stewarts o' Blair will never die.'

So that's what I decided to do. Once people knew I was on the scene again, I got all the bookings I could do. I was booked immediately for the Whitby Folk Festival, and have now performed there for many, many years. It is a big and very enjoyable festival.

One thing that bothered me was the thought of going on the stage on my own for the first time. I found however that it meant I was now my own woman, and I could speak to my audiences for the first time. Up to then my mother always spoke for us. To tell you the truth, I felt reborn. I could sing what I liked and say what I liked. I was liberated for the first time in my life, and it was a great feeling, but it took a long time for me to accept it.

I was driving up to Glen Isla one day, and saw sitting at the roadside a wee girl, so I stopped the car. She was dirty and her clothes were in rags.

'What are you doing here?' I asked her.

'My mammy is up at that ferm getting boiling water for a sup o' tea,' she replied.

I sat down beside her and waited, and soon her mother came down the road from the farm with a teapot in her hand, and she was carrying a bag. She looked at me suspiciously and with a hostile look on her face. 'Who are you?' she asked.

'It's alright, I'm a nackin [traveller],' I replied. 'I was just keeping your wee lassie company, I hope you dinnae mind.'

She looked exhausted, and sat down beside us. 'No, no,' she said, 'you're a nackin, and that's alright. Would you like a cup of tea with us, then?'

'I would love a cup of tea, thanks,' I said.

We sat and had our tea and the scones the farm woman had given her.

'What are you going to do now?' I asked.

'Well, we have a wee tent we can put up for the night,' she said. 'We are not going back to Kirriemuir and that moich [mad] woman we have just left.'

'Which mad woman?' I asked.

'My mither. My, but she is away with the fairies. She's clean aff the heed. I never want to see her again. It will just be me and my wee lassie, Bessie, from now on.'

'You cannae bide up this glen, just the two o' you,' I said.

'No, I am going to Montrose in the morning. I have a sister there. She lives in a wee single end. She is awa' fae her man, and luckily they never had any bairns.'

Before I left the mother and her girl I helped her put up her wee tent, and she built a fire to heat them before they went to bed. I bade them goodbye and carried on my journey.

It was a great thing at that time to be able to go on a journey and still see travellers walking the roads. You would never see that nowadays.

While I am reminiscing on old times I think I will put another wee story in.

My father had a cousin who was a great character. Travellers called him the Highland Chief. His wife's name was Brokie, and they always came to see us when they were in the area. They lived in Dunkeld, in a bow camp up at the slate quarries.

They were Godfearing people. The Chief always went round carrying a Bible. He couldn't read it, but he felt safe with it. They would go into Dunkeld, sing hymns and beg for money. Brokie would be at one side of the road and the Chief was on the other. This particular day they stood there for ages and no one took them on, they had been given nothing.

Now this bien coul (gentleman) came along, and put something in Brokie's hand. The Chief was desperate to know what she had been given, so he sang in cant, so that the folk wouldn't understand them, 'What did the gadgie feek to thee [How much did the man give to you]? Nearer my God to thee.'

Brokie answered, 'The gadgie feekit me one curdee [a halfpenny]. Nearer my God to thee.'

The Chief answered her, 'Tell the gadgie tae bing it in his geer [stick it in his arse]! Nearer my God to thee.'

A few months later Brokie had a baby in the bow tent at the slate quarries. It died, so she ran away and hid herself and the dead baby in another part of the quarry. She was gone for three days, and the Chief couldn't find her.

He went to the police down in Dunkeld and reported her missing, so a squad of policemen went out to try and find her. They found her not too far away from where the bow tent was. She was crying and screaming her head off, and she wouldn't give up the dead baby to them. They finally got it from her, and it was taken and buried near the slate quarries where it was born. Poor wee thing.

I was asked to go and perform in Edinburgh at a school, telling stories to the kids. That was the first school performance I had ever done. I had offered my services to our local school and they said no. The head said my stories wouldn't suit the school. Yet later they took someone else, who told all my stories to the children. Now, if that's not prejudice, what is? Yes, it rears its ugly head now and again, even in this day and age.

A few years ago I was asked to perform in a concert with some of my friends at the Edinburgh Festival – not the Fringe, the official Festival itself. I sang Ewan McColl's song 'Go, Move, Shift'. It was a cracking night.

A few days after I got home, I had a phone call saying I had been chosen as the best singer that week, and had won the Herald Angel award from the *Glasgow Herald*. I had to go back into Edinburgh to receive my certificate and a statue. I got the certificate but I am still waiting for my statue. They said my name had to be engraved on it, so I couldn't get it there and then. My name's not that difficult to spell, so I wonder why I should have had to wait so long.

I have performed in quite a few folk clubs in London, for instance in Peta and Ken Hall's Musical Traditions club, a wonderful traditional club. I have sung there many times. When I left their club the last time I was there, I took the underground and got off at King's Cross station. As I was coming up the last set of stairs into the train station, I was attacked by a mugger. He grabbed my handbag and the trolley suitcase that I was carrying. I lashed out, but he hung on, so I hung on, and yet none of the folk around us tried to help me. I was shouting for help, but I was ignored. This made me angry and I was fuming, so I held on all the tighter. Eventually he threw the two bags at me and ran. I fell backwards, clutching the two bags, onto my arse. It was black and blue for a week.

When I got on the train I had a stiff whisky. I don't drink normally, but I needed a whisky that day. My hips were so sore, and the shock of what had happened had shaken me to the core. As the train left London I conked out and had a good sleep till I got to Carlisle. Please watch out when you go to a big city, take nothing for granted.

One of the worst things that happened to me while I was performing was when I was kidnapped. I was booked to do a storytelling festival at Cape Clear, a small island off the south of Ireland. I had to get the boat from Baltimore to Cape Clear, a 45 minute journey. I landed alright, and stayed with the organiser and his wife, who were Americans. They were wonderful folk. The festival was a great success.

The festival ran from the Friday till Monday morning. I was there till the Tuesday morning and was supposed to fly home out of Cork in the afternoon. Well, that's what I planned, but that is not the way it happened at all.

We were all told we had to get the boat back on the Sunday afternoon, as there was a great storm coming in on the Monday and there would be no sailings. I went to the organiser and told him I wasn't flying out till Tuesday.

'It's alright, Sheila. I have a woman who will put you up in Cork till you are due to fly out,' he said.

An English girl with me was also flying out of Cork on the Tuesday, and the woman, who I'll call Marilyn, said she would put her up as well. So the two of us got on the boat with Marilyn, and once we landed we headed up to Cork.

I was sitting beside Marilyn in the front seat. Halfway there, she turned to me and said, 'Sheila, you do realize I don't stay in Cork, I stay in England, and I am kidnapping you.' She turned to the girl in the back seat and said, 'You just happened to be there, tough!'

I looked back at the girl, and the panic that was in her face was terrible.

'You see, Sheila, I want some people to meet you. They are tree people, and stay 20 minutes north of Cork.'

I looked at her and said, 'What are tree people?'

'They stay in forests protecting the trees from being cut down. Now you have an option. You can sleep in a tent for the night with a wife, husband and their kids, two goats and a few chickens. Or you can sleep up a tree. We have chosen a good tree house for you, don't worry.'

I was panicking, but I knew I must not show it to her. My brain started to go into overdrive. I smiled to myself. I was going to trick her, but I couldn't tell the other girl what I planned or our kidnapper would hear me. So I turned to her and winked, and she smiled. She had caught on, thank God, so she calmed down and stopped fidgeting.

By now we were coming into Cork, and when I saw a few

shops I held my stomach and said to Marilyn, 'I'm going to be sick – quick, stop the car!'

As soon as she pulled up, without thought we opened the door and ran. We had our cases at our feet, so it was no problem to take them.

We ran like the wind up and down a few streets, then I said to the English girl, 'I must stop for a fag.'

We sat down on a bench and collapsed in each other's arms, crying our eyes out. We were so upset we couldn't speak. After I had smoked my fag I felt better, and so did she.

'What we going to do now?' she said.

'Well, we will head in the opposite direction from that mad woman, and I will ask somebody where we can find a bed and breakfast for the night.'

We met a woman on the street and she said there was a hostel just up the road that was much cheaper than a bed and breakfast. So, dragging our suitcases, we went in the direction of the hostel and signed in for the night. We had had nothing to eat all day and felt mentally exhausted. We told the man running the hostel what had happened to us, and he wanted to phone the police, but we said no, we just wanted to forget the whole thing. He made us a cup of tea and some sandwiches, and was our saviour that night, I can tell you.

I have often wondered since then what I would have done if I had been alone. I think the other girl being with me gave me courage. When I got home I couldn't stop thinking about what had happened, and it took me about a week to calm down. I phoned the organiser of the Cape Clear festival and told him I had been kidnapped. He couldn't believe it. I haven't been back to Ireland since.

When I got home there was a letter waiting for me inviting me to do a concert in Aberdeen with my cousin, Stanley Robertson. I loved performing with him – he was a great man, with an unbelievable store of knowledge. He eventually was awarded a doctorate by Aberdeen University.

28
Cathie's Song

A girl called Sadie came to see me one day. I had known her for a few years. She asked for shelter for the night, as in the morning she was heading down to see her parents in Newcastle. She was one of the travelling girls who we would help from time to time.

I made her something to eat, and we sat down with a cup of tea at the fire and started to chat about this and that. She told me about her family, and that her mother was the boss of her father, a thing that was unheard of among travellers. Among travellers the man was always the boss, but not in her family.

'My mother hit my father the other day, and he got four stitches in his brow.'

'Oh my God,' I said, 'How does he stand it? Can he no' leave her?'

She replied, 'He would never do that. It's her that makes the money, and he has nowhere to go. That's why I am going down to see them, because she doesn't hit him when I am there.'

Then she said a funny thing to me. 'Sheila, do you ken the story about the wrestler?'

'Well, I think that's one my father used to tell, God rest his soul.'

'Yes, he did, and I have never forgotten it. It was the best story I had ever heard, especially the way he started it. Your father was a real storyteller. I would like to tell the story to you now as payment for my bed for the night, and you can tell it to other people.'

So we sat there having another cup of tea, and we settled down. It was funny having this girl telling me my father's story.

She began. 'Listen to the introduction,' she said.

The Wrestler
As told by Alex Stewart

Once upon a time, when the birds shit lime, and the monkeys chewed tobacco, there was a family stayed away up in Caithness. They had a laddie and they called him Jeck, and he always used to sit in the ashes at the fire. He was so lazy he never got out of them, and his mother couldn't get baking or cooking because she couldn't get near the fire. She always used to shove him out of the way, but he always crawled back into the ashes again.

Now, there was a market in a place called Wick. A great man used to come there, a wrestler. He used to go through the fair with a sash hanging from his waist and trailing behind him. Any man who lifted the sash would have to wrestle him that day.

So time rolled on till it came to Saturday, which was the market day, and the day of the fair in Wick. Jeck's father was going to the fair, and Jeck asked him where he was going.

'I'm going to Wick, it's market day,' his father said.

'Can I go with you?' Jeck asked.

'Oh laddie, laddie dear, you couldn't walk to Wick, it's too far,' said his father.

Well, there and then Jeck started to cry, although he was a big, big, lump of a boy. Jeck wasn't all there, he was simple. He cried and cried, and his father said to him, 'Well, Jeck, if I take you, you will have to stay beside me, because if you go off through the market, there are so many folk you might get lost.'

'I will, I will,' said Jeck, and off they went.

They got to the market, and walked through the fair, and walked through the fair, and Jeck always stayed beside his father.

Then, when they were walking through the fair, the wrestler went past them, with his sash trailing on the ground. It was yellow, pink and red, all different colours. It was beautiful.

Jeck ran forward and picked up the sash. He said, 'Here, man, pick up your sash, it's trailing on the ground.'

The wrestler clapped the boy on the shoulder, and said, 'You're the man that has to fight me today.' Jeck just laughed and ran back to his father.

'Jeck, why did you do that?' his father said. 'That man will kill you.'

'I can't help it, father, if he kills me or no,' said Jeck. 'His sash was trailing on the ground and getting dirty.'

The day wore on, and there was a ring on a big stage in the middle of the fair where the wrestling match was to take place. Jeck's father went up to the wrestler to have a word with him. 'My son is a simple laddie,' he said. 'You can't wrestle him.'

'I know that,' said the wrestler. 'It's alright, I have another man to wrestle. I said that to the laddie just to frighten him.'

Jeck was standing at the side of the stage. When the wrestler appeared, he took off his coat and jumped into the ring.

When he saw him, his father said, 'Jeck, what are you doing up there, laddie? Come on down from there at once.'

'I have to fight the wrestler,' said Jeck.

'No, no, no, come down out of there,' said his father.

But Jeck said, 'I'm going to fight him. I lifted his sash and I've got to fight him.'

Jeck's father went up to the wrestler and said to him, 'Look, just give him two or three tosses, and he will get fed up and come out of the ring. But please don't hurt him.'

'Alright,' said the wrestler.

Jeck went up to the wrestler, and they were facing in the middle of the ring, going round and round trying to get grips of each other. Jeck caught the man and got his arms in a grip. He was holding him tight. His father started to shout to him, 'Throw him, son, throw him!'

Jeck shouted back to his father, 'I'm feared tae throw him, father, I'm feared tae throw him.'

'Why are you feared tae throw him, Jeck?' asked his father.

'I'll get the jail,' said Jeck.

'Not at all,' said his father, 'throw him!'

So Jeck gave the man a throw, and killed him stone dead. His ribs went right through his heart and through his lungs, and he was smashed to atoms.

So Jeck got the prize money, and I think he will still be champion to this day.

And that's the end of my story.

Sadie looked over at me, and the tears were running down my face. It wasn't Sadie I heard telling me the story, it was my father. She told it exactly like him.

She came over and put her arms round me until I stopped crying. 'Now it's your turn,' she said to me.

'What do you mean?' I asked.

'I need something from you to take away with me.'

'But what?' I asked.

'Oh, Sheila, a song, of course.'

'Which one?' I asked her.

'The last one you sang to my family round our camp-fire,' she said.

'I can't remember which one it was.'

'Well, I do,' she answered. 'It was your version of the night-visiting song, I love it.'

'Very well,' I replied, 'but I haven't sung it since my auld mother died.'

We settled down and I started to sing it.

The Night-Visiting Song

Here's a health to all true lovers,
And here's to mine, wherever she may be,
This very night I will go and see her,
Although she is many's a long mile from me.

Let the night be dark as the very dungeon,
Let not a star shine from above,
But I will be guided, oh saftly guided,
Into the arms of my own true love.

He then approached her bedroom window,
His knee he placed on a cold damp stone,
Through the pane of glass he gently whispered,
'My darling maid, do you sleep alone?'

She raised her head from her soft white pillow,
And her hand she placed o'er her lily white breast,
Through the pane of glass she gently whispered,
'Who is this that disturbs my quiet night's rest?'

''Tis only I, my darling lover,
Open the door, love, and let me in,
For I am tired of this long night's journey,
And besides I am drenched to the very skin.'

She opened the door with the greatest of pleasure,
She opened the door and he walked in,
They both embraced, and they kissed each other,
Till the dawning of day it came creeping in.

'The cocks are crowing, my love, I must be going,
The cocks are crowing, and I must obey,
The cocks are crowing, love, I must be going,
For we are but servants and we must obey.'

Now I had to comfort Sadie. Why do we cry when we enjoy things? My mother always said it was the emotions in you coming out.

The next day Sadie left about 11 o'clock. That was years ago, and I have never heard from her since. I always wondered whether she had died, because it wasn't like her not to keep in touch. Well, she's where God pleases now, I suppose. I do know her mother died, and she herself lost a wee boy of three, and became a recluse after that.

My sister Cathie had a stroke, and was rushed into Perth Infirmary. She lost her speech and couldn't walk. She was in there for months. Eventually she improved, she could talk and walk again, and so she was transferred to an old folk's home in Blairgowrie.

I went to see her a lot, and took her out in the car sometimes. The head nurse told me she had a series of wee strokes that gave her a tremor and made her balance not so good.

She was a few years in the home, and then one day I got a phone call to say she wasn't too well, and could I come out to her. She was in bed when I arrived, and there was a hazy look in her eyes. The nurse said she couldn't speak or communicate with the staff, and she had stopped eating.

I took her hand and said to her, 'Cathie, it's me, Sheila.' No response from her.

I thought to myself, she isn't getting to go without knowing me. I looked at her lying there, and said to myself, don't cry just now, wait till later.

I gripped her hand and said to her, 'Cathie, I want you to sing me a song, your favourite,' and I started it. After the first verse, she joined me in a whisper and gripped my hand, and we both finished the song, all four verses of it. Here is the song:

John Mitchell

I am a true-born Irishman, John Mitchell is my name,
And for to join my countrymen, from Newry town I came,
I struggled hard both day and night, to free my native land,
From which I was transported, unto Van Diemen's Land.

When first I joined my countrymen, it was in '42,
And what did follow after, I will now explain to you,
I raised the standard of revolt, and I gloried in the deed,
And I vowed to heaven I ne'er would rest, till old
                                        Ireland would be freed.

While here in prison close confined, await my trial day,
My loving wife she came to me, and this to me did say,
'Oh John, my dear, keep up your heart, and daunted
                                        never be,

For it's better to die for Ireland's rights, than to live
in slavery.'

When I received my sentence, in irons I was bound,
When hundreds of my countrymen were rallied all around,
There's one request I'll ask of you, when liberty you gain,
Just think of poor John Mitchell, who now wears a
convict's chain.

When we had finished singing, I then asked her, 'Do you ken who I am?' and she replied, in a louder voice, 'Sheila, my sister.'

I ran out at that and had a good cry, and that was the last time I saw her alive. But she will never leave me, ever. She is in my heart, and that's where she will stay.

We had the funeral, and she was buried with her husband Jimmy. For the life of me, I can't remember her funeral. It's as if I have blocked it out of my mind.

Well, that was the last of my brothers and sisters, and I was left alone to struggle with my memories. Each of them in their own way was special to me. They were the last travellers on my wavelength and my life now will never be the same again.

29
Jess and Other Friends

I have a few best friends who I would like to mention in this book. One of them is Jess Smith, who got me writing in the first place. She said, 'Sheila, you have a book in you,' and she was right. Thanks, Jess!

I had known Jess when she was very young, but we lost contact. After very many years we met up again at Alness in Ross-shire. I was doing a weekend festival there with Stanley Robertson, Alex John Williamson and Essie Stewart. Jess and Davie, her husband, were in the audience. I was so pleased to see her and Davie again after such a long time. There were other travellers there as well. It fairly boosts your morale when travellers are there to support you.

When I was due to come home, Jess and Davie gave me a lift in their wee van. Jess was relegated to the back of the van. On the way down, she told me all that was happening to her life. She had become an author. 'Wow!' I thought.

I turned round to her and said, 'Jess, do you sing?'

'No' me, Sheila, I don't sing.'

'Why not?' I asked.

'No reason, I just don't sing.'

'Well,' I said, 'you will be a singer before we get home. Let me hear you sing, Jess.'

She grumbled a bit about this, but Davie said to her, 'Go on, Jess, sing.'

And so she did.

I waited till she had finished and turned to her. 'You are singing like Deanna Durbin – you are too polite.'

Then I sang a verse of a song to her in the traditional travellers' way. That day I taught her a ballad, and showed her how to sing it. She was a quick learner, and had the song by heart before we got to Blair. Since then she has never looked back. Here is the ballad I taught her.

The Nobleman

A nobleman lived in a mansion,
And he courted his own servant maid,
'Twas neither for love nor for beauty,
But only to lead her astray.

So one night as he entered her bedroom,
As Mary was losing her stays,
''Tis many fine presents I'll give you,
One night for to lie by your side.'

'Oh, master, I wonder to hear you,
A man of such honour and pride,
To ask a poor innocent lassie,
One night for to lie by your side.

For if I was to fall with a baby,
'Twould be the very first thing you'd deny,
And me and my baby would perish,
And you in your mansion would lie.'

'Now if you were to fall with a baby,
'Twould be the very first thing I would do,
I would write out a cheque for some money,
And build a fine cottage for you.'

But he saw that he couldn't get round her,
So he said he would make her his bride,
So now she's a nobleman's lady,
And lies by a nobleman's side.

When Jess told me I had a book in me, I asked her and her good man Davie, 'What kind of book?'

'What kind of book do you think you want to write, Sheila?' she asked.

'A book about my mother,' I replied.

'Well, write her biography,' said Jess.

I was so pleased when, a couple of years later, my mother's biography, *Queen Amang the Heather*, came out. I just hope I did my mother justice in the book.

A few academics had wanted to write the life of my mother. When they approached me about it, they said that my mother was such a lady it needed an academic to write about her. I looked at them and said, 'Who knew my mother better than me?'

'That's true,' they said, 'but you're not educated enough to be an author.'

One of them said to me, 'I don't know why all you travellers want to be authors anyway.'

I answered, 'What do you mean, all us travellers?'

'Well, there is you, Stanley [Robertson], Jess [Smith] and Duncan [Williamson]. You travellers should keep your place in society.' Those were the exact words used.

I was really upset and hurt by this remark. I had thought this person was my friend, but that wasn't the case. The academics don't want us to succeed in any educational area where they think they should be in charge.

There is one thing I do know, my mother's life story has been selling well, and that's all that matters to me.

My mother always said that travellers were the 'pilgrims of the mist'. I used this as the title for my second book, a collection of short stories I had gathered from other travellers. They had so many good stories to tell I wanted to get them published also. I thought *Pilgrims of the Mist* was a great title, and so did the publisher, Birlinn.

Jess and I were invited to go to Montrose to take part in a memorial concert for Betsy Whyte, one of the finest traveller writers. I felt proud at being asked to do it. Betsy was a great friend of my family, and she was born in Rattray. It was a great concert.

When I came home that night I found a note pushed through my letterbox. I was astonished at what it said.

> Hello Sheila, this is Sheila who was named after you when I was born in the bow tent at Kirriemuir. I wanted to see you. My mother is with me, but my dad died a few years ago. I will call again tomorrow, about twelve.
>
> Love Sheila xxx

I had to sit down, I was so excited. I couldn't wait till the next day.

On the stroke of 12, a knock came to my door, and there stood Sheila and her mother. Oh my goodness, but Sheila was beautiful. She was dressed very smartly, and so was her mother. Before I could say anything, she ran to me and threw her arms around my neck. She was crying, and so was I.

I brought them into the house, and we had some tea. Their car was parked outside, not a new one but a very nice one.

'Well, well,' I said, 'and you have a car now?'

'I bought it from Snookum's garage, and it's no' a bad wee car. But guess what?' Sheila's mother said, 'We are emigrating to Canada next week! It's all set up. We leave on Tuesday. I have another coul [man], you know, and he has money. I met him at Crieff games a year ago. Sheila, we are so happy about this, but we couldn't go over there before Sheila had met you. Now she is content. God bless you, Sheila, for all you have done for us. Take care of yourself.'

They left to go on their travels. Two months later, I got word they had landed alright, and were settling in fine.

30
Illness and Recovery

❧

I often look back on my life now, and when I think of the poverty we went through, it sometimes doesn't feel real. Like when we went into a turnip field at night, took turnips and boiled them for food. We didn't realise they weren't purple tops, they were yellow tops, what we used to call cattle neeps. They were foul and horribly sweet, but must is a good master. We paid for them the next day. They ran the guts out of us.

I also remember the time we were starving, and my husband Ian went and stole two chickens from a nearby farm. He got home and we skinned them and put them in a big pot I had. An hour later, a knock came to the door, and two policemen were standing there.

'Ian, we have come to arrest you for stealing chickens,' they said.

So they took him away. As they were going out of the door, one of the policemen looked back and said to me, 'Don't let the chickens burn, now.' Then it struck me that they could smell them cooking. Down at the station they found a feather in Ian's pocket, and he was fined.

Here is a story my mother told me, and she swore it was true. Once I asked her, 'How do you know it's true?'

She replied, with a smirk on her face, 'Because, Sheila, as you well know, travellers don't tell lies,' and she started her story.

The Burn That Ran Wine

My granny used to tell this story about a wee burn in one of the glens. It ran past a farmhouse, and there was a wee cotter house near the farm, and two old sisters and a brother stayed in the wee cotter house.

Now, as poor as they were, they still kept Hogmanay night. They cleaned their house from top to bottom to have it ready for 12 o'clock, and lifted out the ashes from the fireplace.

Once everything had been done for Hogmanay, one of the sisters said to the other, 'Look, it's nearly 12, and we have no water. It will be gey hard for you to get back with it in time. You had better hurry – you go for it and I will set the table.' There was a wee spring near the burn where they got their water, and they carried it back in wooden buckets.

The sister who was going for the water didn't want to miss midnight and have to be the first foot, she wanted to be in the house when the bells rang.

She hurried along beside the burn to get to the spring. Before she reached the spring she dipped one of the buckets into the burn to rinse it out, then emptied the water back into the burn. She dipped the other bucket into the burn and was about to empty it out, when her eye caught sight of it in the clear moonlight. She was shocked to see that it was a different colour to normal water. However she had no time to ponder about it, as it was near 12. Instead of going on to the spring to fill her buckets, she kept the burn water in her bucket and went home.

When she got back to the house with the strange water, they looked at it and examined it and smelled it. Finally the brother came forward with a cup and dipped it in. 'That's no' water,' he said. Then he took a drink of it, and it turned out to be wine. On the table was a bucket of wine. Either one minute before, or one minute after midnight, that particular burn had run wine. The two old sisters and the brother had a great Hogmanay that year.

Now that was spoken about for a long time in the glen, but nobody ever was there by the burn at that exact time again.

When I was small and my mother told me that travellers never told lies, I fully believed it. As I got older, I said to myself, if we didn't lie how could we ever have survived for generations? That was my bubble well and truly burst, and I felt sad.

One morning I woke up and I was covered all over with big welts like blisters all over my body, and they were itching terribly. I went to the doctor and was sent to Ninewells hospital. They did many tests in the first week and discovered I was diabetic. The inflamed skin patches were caused by urticaria.

To clear this up I had to have baths twice a day, with a special solution in the water, and then to cover the whole of my body with a medicinal cream. I had to lie on a sponge mattress on top of my hospital one. I also had to wash my hair with a special medicated shampoo. This treatment helped the itch a wee bit, but I still couldn't sleep at night. With this and the diabetes I was very ill. I kept being sick and couldn't eat, even though they put me on a diabetic diet. I just wanted to drink water all the time.

After two weeks I was not getting better, so they decided to put me into a box like a tanning machine that beamed ultra-violet light down on the urticaria, but for only five minutes at a time. I still had to bathe twice a day. Because I was really sick and could hardly walk for tiredness, it was a terrible chore for me to get into the bath and out of it. I often thought to myself, 'Here I am in hospital again. The last time was for seven months, surely I won't be in as long now, oh God, no.'

My kids came in every day to see me. I know they were worried to death about me. After three weeks in my bed I was no further forward, only getting up to use the toilet and go for the blue light sessions.

What kept me sane in there was a woman from Blair called May, she was so comical. She was in with another type of skin trouble. I was in a sorry state, I can tell you. It wasn't till the fifth week that the itch completely disappeared, and the welts started to shrink a bit. The illness had dragged me down a lot, but it was good when I was not quite so exhausted going to take my baths.

I was six weeks in the hospital and it felt like six months. That was when I missed my mother and father the most, not having them visit me in hospital, because they would have been in every day.

I got home from the hospital finally, but the baths and the cream on my body still continued. I have been fine ever since. The doctor in Ninewells said my illness was due to a blood condition, combined with the diabetes.

After I came home from hospital I suddenly remembered a story my granny had told me. I had forgotten about it, but my illness with the spots all over me reminded me of it.

There was a girl who her family called Pigeon, though her real name was Betsy, because she was so thin and delicate and just picked at her food. She was a shy girl.

The family were putting up their tent near Fortingall one year when the farmer arrived and asked them if they would do some work for him helping with the harvest. Glad of the work, they said yes.

There was another family there as well, staying in a wee cotter house that belonged to the farmer. So there was a father, mother, two sons and Pigeon, and with the folk in the house the farmer had a good squad. They were due to start work the next day.

The family that stayed in the cotter house were horrible to the travellers. What made them worse was that the travellers did twice the work that they did, and they got praised for it. The jealousy of the cotter family was terrible. They were supposed to supply the travellers with water, but they refused to give them any. This meant that the travellers had to walk two miles to the nearest stream for water. They didn't let on to the farmer, however.

This went on for a few days. Then Pigeon was taken ill, with spots all over her body, big welts like blisters similar to the ones I had.

That Sunday the travellers had a cousin and her man come over to see them for a visit. The cousin's nickname was Turnaboot Katie, and her man was Hector. The travellers gave Katie that name because she was always changing her mind about everything. She was a nice creature, but moich (soft in the head), or so my granny said. It all happened before my granny's time, and it was her mother who had told her the story.

Katie and Hector came into the camp, and the family was glad to see them. They all sat round the fire and had a cup of tea.

'Where's Pigeon?' Katie asked.

'She is asleep in the tent, I don't want to wake her.'

'I can't go away without seeing my wee Pigeon,' said Katie. She went into the tent, then started screaming and ran back out of the tent again.

'Oh, my God, my God,' she said, 'What's wrong with her?'

'We don't know,' said Pigeon's mother. 'She just took ill and came out in all these big blistery spots.'

'It's the plague that lassie has got,' shouted Katie, 'you are all going to die!' and she made off with her man behind her.

When the folk in the cotter house saw Katie and Hector running by, they stopped her and asked her what was wrong. She told them what she had seen, and said that it was the plague that Pigeon had. The woman in the house started to panic, and flew up to the farm to tell the farmer.

He came rushing down and asked the travellers what the hell was wrong. When they told him, he said, 'I will get my horse and cart, and she can sit in the back of it, and I will take her to the doctor. You can all stay here, I don't want all of you plaguing my cart.'

Pigeon's father carried her out wrapped in a sack, and put her in the back of the cart. The farmer sped off down the track road.

Time passed and there was no sign of them coming back. Pigeon's mother and father were so worried they were pacing up and down, unable to settle.

After a few hours, down the road came the farmer, but there was no Pigeon with him.

'Where is my lassie?' asked the father.

'Oh, she is safe,' said the farmer, and would tell them nothing else about what had happened. All he said to them was, 'I want you tinks off my land now, and I mean now.'

Shocked and worried about their girl, the mother started crying and the man tried to console her, to no avail.

So they packed up their belongings, put them in the pram they used to carry their things, and went up to the farm to see if the farmer would tell them more about Pigeon. He refused to say anything else about the girl, where he had taken her or anything. He gave them what small amount of money was coming to them for the harvest work, and chased them off his land.

That was the last time anybody ever saw or heard of Pigeon. The family went to the police, who, of course, said they knew nothing about her. Some folk say the farmer sold Pigeon to be used for experiments. All I know is that my granny said she was never heard tell of again.

Now what I was thinking when I remembered this story, maybe I am wrong, but perhaps she was sold to science, and experiments on her may have helped to get a cure for me. I hope not, but you never can tell.

31
The Big C

❧

I wish I could say my hospital time was over, but no, it was not. One day I had a shower and discovered a lump in my left breast. Not a small one, a big one, and it was painful. I told no one for weeks. Then I noticed it was getting bigger, so I told my daughter, Heather, and she made me go to the doctor.

A week later I was in Perth Royal Infirmary for a biopsy. After it was taken, we had to wait to see if the growth was malignant or not. We went and sat in the waiting room until the doctor called us into his office. He told me it was cancer, and that there were two large lumps, one on top of the other.

I looked at him and said, 'What happens now?'

He was very sad and apologetic, but said I needed an operation to have the breast removed.

'Alright,' I said, 'just whip it off. I have had it long enough now anyway.'

The professor looked at me strangely. He thought I would be crying and bubbling, but I was as calm as could be.

The doctor said to my daughter, 'Your mother is the bravest woman I have ever met.'

It was just that I was brought up to accept anything that God sends you. What's the use of crying? It only upsets the people around you. And I am not a weak woman.

So I said to him, 'When are you going to whip it off, then, doctor?'

He laughed and replied, 'Next week.'

I said, 'Right oh,' and went home.

The worst part of it was telling my kids and friends that I had cancer.

I must admit the thought went through my mind, 'Well, this is what I am going to die of – cancer!' Or the big C, as folk called it.

A week passed and I went into the hospital for my operation. I went in one day and had my operation the next. Heather came in with me, but before the operation I told her just to go home and phone in. However when I awoke after the anaesthetic I was back in my bed, and Heather was holding my hand. I can't describe the huge feelings of relief I had when I opened my eyes and she was there. It was not an uncomfortable operation. I felt fine physically, it was more the thinking about what had happened that bothered me.

I was in the Infirmary for ten days and then got home, but a few days later I was taken into Blairgowrie Cottage Hospital. It had taken all that time for it to sink in that I had cancer. When it did, I couldn't cope with it. I wouldn't take a bath, because I couldn't bear to look at the wound left by the operation. That was the reason they put me back into hospital. I was very pleased, because I wasn't able to cope with it at home. The nurses were so nice, and I knew them all. I got masses of flowers from my folk-singer friends, the big ward was like the garden of Eden.

I was now feeling uncomfortable all the time. A few days the doctor had to pump fluid off the wound. This procedure wasn't painful, but it felt to me when they did it as though they were pumping away the cancer out of my system. They weren't, of course, but at that time I was vulnerable to all kinds of illogical thoughts. The nurses had to shower me because I still wouldn't look at where my breast used to be. The doctor said I was in shock, and it would take a while for me to accept the loss of part of me. I was in the hospital for six weeks, and at the end of that time had got over my shock, and was able to accept my one-boob body.

A friend came to see me in hospital just before I was due to come out. She said the funniest thing to me, and it made me completely relax. 'Sheila, when you come out,' she said, 'we will go on the internet and look for a one-armed man for you.' Afterwards I giggled all day. When people gave me sympathy after the operation I used the same line on them, and it worked in cheering them up too.

Once I was back at home, Heather and me had to go into Perth Hospital again so that I could be measured for a false boob. I was so embarrassed, but got the measurements taken and came home. A week later a big box arrived. I knew what was in the box, and put off opening it, but my mind was on it all day.

Heather phoned me and asked if my chicken fillet had arrived yet. I burst out laughing, and said it had. 'Well, what's it like?' she asked.

I said I did not know, as I had been ignoring it all day.

'Go and open it now,' she told me.

When I opened it I let a scream out of me. Heather was shouting at me down the phone, asking me what was wrong. I couldn't answer. So she jumped into her car and came down to my house. I was still sitting with the phone in my hand and laughing my head off.

'Heather,' I said, 'they have sent me a cow's elder [udder]. It is so big I can't lift it out of the box!'

She looked at it and burst out laughing. 'Mum, neither can I.'

They had sent me the wrong size. We couldn't look at it again for laughing. I said, 'It must have cost them a fortune in postage,' and that set us off laughing again.

We went in to the Infirmary the next day and showed them the false boob. The woman in the department laughed herself when she saw it. She said, 'That would give you some sore back carrying that around with you all day,' and we all laughed again. I hope you men don't read about this, it is for women's eyes only.

That was three times I was in hospital, with three diseases. I have had a rough life as far as illness is concerned. After a while I got the all-clear with my cancer, but you never can tell. No one knows for sure if it will ever come back. I hope not. If it does, I will have to look on the internet for a man with no arms. What else can you do but make a joke about it? If you see the funny side, it is good medicine for the body.

I am so glad my mother and father were not there by that time, or my husband Ian. I think I would have been even more devastated if they had been around. But my kids were a great support to me and I coped fine.

I cope in a funny way sometimes. If I get depressed, I go to my room and sing a ballad, but when I am singing I hear my uncle Donald's or my mother's voice, never my own. Their travellers' ways are ingrained into me, and I can't help it.

There was one verse of a song that constantly milled around in my brain while I was in my bed with cancer. It always makes me laugh.

> If you have the toothache, and greetin' wi' the pain,
> Dinnae buy bags o' sweeties, for that's a silly game,
> Fill your mouth wi' water and mix wi' castor oil,
> And put your arse upon the fire till it begins to boil.

Thoughts like that always came to me. When I was ill I also thought a lot about memories of the past.

My family always used to go and camp where the work was, at harvest time for example. We would be there to scythe the corn, tying it in bunches and stooking it. We looked forward to the camp, because we knew there would be other travellers there also doing the harvest, and we would have great fun together.

One day we went to a place near Alyth, about five miles away, and sure enough, when we got there, there was a family already camped. It was my father's cousin, his wife and their 13 bairns (yes, 13! They had big families in those days).

After we got our tent up we heard someone else coming into the field. It was two other travellers, a mother and her daughter. The old woman would be about 60, and her daughter in her late 30s. My father helped them to put up their tent. When I went over to see if I could give them a hand, I noticed both of them were completely bald. This gave me a shock as you can imagine, but they were the nicest women you could ever meet.

That night we had a big sing-song round the fire, and told ghost stories. The kids were so frightened that they would not go to their beds. So the father, my dad's cousin, made them lie side by side on the ground, took the tent and pulled it over them, and they slept till morning.

The first pay day was a great occasion. The man and his wife and kids decided they would go to Dundee to buy some things with the money. When they got up in the morning, however, there was no water in the can to make their tea apart from about one cup full. Instead of making tea they decided to wash their faces in the can. Each of them dipped a finger into the can, wet it and wiped their eyes, and as far as they were concerned that was them washed. Then they headed off to Dundee.

When I think back to the times we had sitting round the fire with other travellers, speaking our cant language, singing and telling stories, that is the thing I miss most in my life. However, I suppose we have to change with the times.

I remember we were at the berries one day. I was carrying my bucket up to be weighed when a fight broke out. A man said he was being short-changed by the cashier. So the gaffer, who wasn't a traveller, came to see what was going on. The man was very cheeky to the gaffer, and jumped up onto to the lading bank where the berries were weighed.

The gaffer lifted his fist and gave him a colossal punch. The man staggered back and fell into a barrel of berries. You can imagine what he looked like when he got up, because the berries were going to make dye.

When we arrived at the berryfields the next morning, all the barrels in the field had been burned in a huge bonfire. I wonder who did that?

You might be wondering why I am putting all these wee stories into my autobiography. This is what I have done all my life. We travellers are always speaking about the past, and when we remember things we like to tell them as stories. I don't want to miss out anything that has been important in my life. I am now 73, and a huge amount of water has gone under the bridge since I was born.

Here is another story my father used to tell. My son Ian now tells it in the same way. I think it is appropriate here because it is about berries.

The Jam Maker
As told by Alex Stewart

There was once a man who worked as a gardener at a big house. He was very good at growing all kinds of berries – strawberries, raspberries, blackcurrants, redcurrants and everything like that.

He made jam from the berries for the big house. He was an all-round gardener and fruit man, but he wasn't too pleased with his standard of life and was looking for a better job. He wasn't married or anything like that, so there was nothing keeping him where he was.

One day he saw a job advertisement in the paper. It said 'Gardener and Jam-Maker Wanted, only genuine tradesmen need apply.' The job was overseas; in fact in China. The wages were good and full board was provided.

He wrote away to the address that was given, and got a letter back with a ticket for travel to China, and some money as well. The letter gave details of the town in China where he had to go, and he was told to report to a particular shop when he got there. So he gave his notice to his old employers, and went off to China.

When he got to China, he went to the wee shop where he had been told to go. There he found an old Chinese man, who told him he had to go to a place inland about 40 or 50 miles away. The man in the shop said he would take him there in a horse-drawn cart.

When they finally got there, the Chinese man stopped at the end of the road and pointed to a house nearby. 'That's the house you are looking for over there,' he said.

In he went through a gate, and came to a small cottage. It was a lovely cottage and he greatly admired it. He went up to the door and knocked on it, but there was no answer. He knocked again, and looked all around, but nobody was there. He tried the door and it opened. Inside he found that a fire was lit, and the table set, and there were instructions on the table just to make himself at home, and to start work right away.

Next to the cottage there was a garden and a jam-making shed with boilers in it. He needed a rest after his journey, so he did not start work until the next day. All the tools and anything that a gardener needed was there. In the shed were bags and bags of the finest sugar, and wonderful copper boilers for making the jam. He had to pick the fruit from the trees and bushes, and put it in the boilers to make the jam.

Every night when he was finished work and went back to the cottage, the table was always set and food was ready for him. When he got up in the morning the table was set for breakfast.

He soon started to wonder about this, because he never saw another soul, not a single human being, all the time he was there.

One night he came in, got his supper, and went to bed. All of a sudden he could feel a strange sensation come over him, and the bed started to shake. He tried to hang on, but when he opened his eyes he found he was standing outside. In front of him there was a blue light like a will o' the wisp about the size of a bicycle lamp. He heard a voice saying, 'Grasp the blue light.'

So he started to run after the light – through bushes, into ditches, through streams and bumping into trees until he was exhausted. The light was flickering here and flickering there. He tried to jump on it, but as soon as he got near it, it scooted away and was further away than ever.

Then he woke up, to find himself in his bed, tossing and turning and wrestling with his two pillows. He was so tired that he was late starting his work the next morning.

The next night the same thing happened – the bed started to shake and in a moment he was outside. Again the blue light was there in front of him. It moved here, there and everywhere – in fields, across water, in woods, in and out of quarries, and all the while he chased it, and chased it, and chased it. At last he came to a river, a wide, smooth river, and the light went across and over to the other side. You would think it was deliberately tantalising him.

The gardener dived into the river, but discovered to his horror that it was boiling lava instead of water. It was flowing down from a burning volcano, right down to the place where he had jumped in. He could feel his legs starting to melt with the heat of the lava.

He managed to get over to the far side, and made another grab at the light, but it danced away in front of him again.

Then he woke up and found he was wrestling and struggling with the pillows in his own bed. He was completely exhausted. He had a smoke and said to himself, 'Oh my God, if I don't get out of here soon I am going to be found dead. I don't know what's wrong with this place.'

But every morning when he got up he became enchanted with the place again, and he said to himself, 'I will just give it another try.'

Then the next night the bed started shaking, and he was outside chasing the blue light again. This time he thought to himself, 'I am not going to run so fast tonight.' Instead of running, he walked after the blue light. Now it went another way, along a different road altogether.

Finally they reached a big old ruin like a monastery. It had no roof, just walls. He walked in through the main door and there was a wide staircase going up in front of him. Everything was lit up, and there were dozens of people in old-fashioned Chinese clothes, ladies with noblemen like courtiers, going to and fro. The blue light went up the stairs, and the gardener followed it.

He came into a big ballroom upstairs where a crowd of people were dancing to music, and the blue light circled round them. The gardener ran after it, but failed to catch it as usual. Finally he stood in a corner, weighing everything up.

In the room was the most beautiful girl he had ever seen, and the music was so good he decided to ask her to dance. As soon as he started dancing with her, he heard a loud 'Tramp! Tramp! Tramp!' and the whole building started to shudder. Everybody stopped dancing and huddled by the walls of the room. In through the door came a huge black stallion, with a rider on its back. If ever there was a devil, this was him. The horse came right out into the middle of the ballroom floor.

Between the horse's legs the blue light was hovering. The gardener made a dive through the horse's legs and caught the blue light.

At that moment he woke up. He was fighting with his pillows again, hanging half out of the bed. He fell onto the floor and lay there panting.

Then he heard a knock on the door. 'Come in,' he said.

In came three men dressed in servants' livery. 'At your service, Your Majesty,' they said to him, 'We are here to wait on you.'

The gardener said to them, 'What do you mean by calling me Your Majesty?'

The servants ignored his comment, and said, 'Come on, Your Majesty, we are here to get you dressed up.'

Just then another man stepped in, clothed in the finest princely robes. 'You are getting married this morning,' he announced.

'You are making a mistake, lads. I am the gardener here. I'm the man that makes the jam.'

He was still arguing and trying to resist, but they managed to get him to put the clothes on that they had brought.

When he went outside, he found that soldiers were standing to attention all along the road from his wee house to the big ruin that he had run to the night before. The ruin had now changed into a great castle. Trumpets were blowing and bands were playing. The gardener was driven in an ornate carriage right up to the castle door.

When he arrived there, the beautiful girl was waiting for him. She was a princess.

'Look here,' said the gardener, 'this is a mistake. I'm the man from the gardener's cottage down the road.'

'You are the man who came here last night, and grasped the blue light, and broke the enchantment that had been put on us by the Devil,' said the princess. She explained everything that had happened to him, and how he had rescued the country from the spell that it had been under. The two of them got married and lived happily ever after.

And that's the end of my story.

32
A Visit to the Palace

❧

I received a letter one day from Buckingham Palace. I was afraid to open it. I phoned my son Gregor, and he came down and opened it for me.

'Mum,' he said, 'you have been awarded the MBE by the Queen.'

I started to shake. I thought to myself that there must be a mistake, that it couldn't possibly be me. But it was true. I was going to be given the MBE in the Queen's Birthday Honours.

I was told I had to keep quiet about it until they released the news to the papers. It was three months before this happened, but I had told everyone long before. It was too important a thing to keep to myself.

Once I had been notified, I was inundated with letters from London. One came from the prime minister, and there were others from high-up people at the Palace with instructions about what I had to wear, how I should behave etc. etc. I had never been as nervous before in my life, even when I had met the Queen in Washington. Ah, but I was younger then, and took things in my stride.

I decided to take Heather, my daughter, Hamish, my son, and Roy to the Palace to watch me receive the honour. We went down the night before, and booked into a hotel near the Palace. We had a taxi ordered the next morning to take us to the ceremony.

We had a pass to get us into the Palace. We were ushered through the front door into a huge hallway, and had to go up the most beautiful staircase I have ever seen. Standing at the top of the stairs were the Beefeaters. It made my Heather jump when she walked up the stairs and suddenly caught sight of them.

When we got to the top of the staircase, my kids went left, and I went right. I was taken into a vast room, like a 'green room' with nibbles and drinks. The paintings in that room were unbelievable – real oil paintings worth a few fortunes, I bet. I had a sit down on every chair in the room, including one that Queen Victoria had sat on. I felt really important at that moment, but when I got up I thought to myself, 'Sheila, you are still a traveller.'

A few male attendants appeared, and the head one spoke to us. He explained the ceremony we had to go through to receive the honour. He told us where to stand when we got to the ballroom, and that when our names were called out we had to walk forward, curtsey, then go up and have our medal pinned on. The only drawback was that the Queen couldn't be there, as she had a sore back, and it was to be Prince Charles instead. I was so happy it was him. He knew about me and Scottish travellers.

After this, the man demonstrated how we should curtsey, and showed the men what they had to do, a short bow. One of the other attendants pinned small hooks on our chests so that the Prince would be able to hang the medals on them.

Each of us was called individually to receive our medals. I walked up to Prince Charles and curtsied. He said to me, 'Sheila, I know all about you. It is about time the travelling people were given an award for keeping the culture of Scotland alive.'

I replied, 'But Your Highness, we used to be called tinkers, don't forget that.'

He burst out laughing, and said, 'Well done, Sheila!' He also said to me, 'You are a folk-singer and storyteller.'

'Yes,' I replied.

'Well,' he said, 'If there was no one else here I would have you up on that stage, singing and telling me a story.'

Then he pinned the medal on and shook my hand.

There were a lot of photos taken when I was speaking to the Prince, and I have them all. I even have a video of me receiving my medal with my family which the Palace sent me. It is something I will always treasure.

It was a long day, and by the end, after all the excitement, we were exhausted. We caught the train home, and dozed all the way home to Perth.

When I got home all my folk-singer friends phoned me to see how I had got on. My tongue was sore telling everyone the same story, but it was great to share it with them.

I was still getting bookings to sing and tell stories, and after I got the medal I got even more. I will tell you the hardest thing for me about it all – it was putting MBE after my name. The first letter I got with Sheila Stewart MBE on it, I must admit, I was shamed to death. Why, I don't know. I think it is probably just my shy nature, and partly that after being looked down on for so long, it was difficult to imagine me – a traveller! – receiving such an honour. It was like a dream to me.

The thing that annoyed me, was that it was England that gave me the honour. What would Scotland give me? Nothing, and that hurt. I know we are in the United Kingdom, and so the MBE came from Scotland as well. But it wasn't the same to me as getting something from Scotland itself. But later on I was to eat my words about that.

People have asked me since, if I had sung to the Prince, what would I have sung. I puzzled with this for a long time, and then I said to myself, 'The Bonny Hoose o' Airlie'. That is the song I sang for his parents and the US president in Washington. It was my mother's song, and it goes like this.

Bonny Hoose o' Airlie

It fell on a day, a bonny summer's day,
When the corn was ripe and yellow,
That there fell oot a great dispute,
Between Argyle and Airlie.

Lady Margaret looked ower yon high castle wa',
And oh, but she sighed sairly,
When she saw Argyle and a' his men
Come to plunder the bonny hoose o' Airlie.

'Come doon, come doon, Lady Margaret,' he said,
'Come doon and kiss me fairly,
Or gin the mornin's clear delight,
I winna leave a standin stane in Airlie.'

'If my guid lord had a been at hame,
But he's awa' wi' Cherlie,
There wouldnae come a Campbell fae Argyle
Dare trod upon the bonny green o' Airlie.

For I hae bore him seven bonny sons,
And the eighth yin has never seen his daddy,
But if I had as mony o'er again,
They would a' be men for Cherlie.'

But poor Lady Margaret was forced tae come doon,
And oh, but she sighed sairly,
And there in front o' a' his men,
She was ravished on the bowlin' green o' Airlie.

Argyle, in a rage, he kindled sich a low,
All o'er the lift so red and clearly,
And poor Lady Margaret, and a' her wains
Were smothered in the dark reek o' Airlie.

'Draw yer dirks, draw yer dirks,' cried the brave Locheil,
'Unsheathe yer sword,' cried Cherlie,
'For I'll kindle sich a low roond the false Argyle,
And I'll licht it wi' a spark oot o' Airlie.'

33
Travellers till the End

❧

I had to eat my words about Scotland not giving me an honour. I was mistaken. After I arrived home from London, I got a phone call saying I was to be inducted into the Scottish Traditional Music Hall of Fame in Fort William – would I accept it, and come up to the presentation? I said of course I would accept it.

I asked Jess and Davie Smith if they would come with me. Davie drove us up on the day of the presentation. It was in a big hotel in Fort William. We were shown into the huge ballroom and the front beside the stage was full of tables with white tablecloths, bottles of wine and boxes of chocolates on them. The atmosphere was like the Oscars, it was wonderful. You are entered into the Hall of Fame as a recognition for all you have put into traditional music throughout your life. I have now been 55 years on the traditional music scene, spreading my travellers' culture. I received a card and a beautiful trophy shaped like a vase, with my name on it, and an inscription saying why I had got it.

A few months ago I got an email from Donald Smith, the director of the Storytelling Centre in Edinburgh. The seats in the theatre were being named to honour outstanding individuals, and he wanted to present me with one with my name on it. He also said in the email that I should be given a BA.

I puzzled over this for a few days. I couldn't ask Donald because he was on holiday. A friend told me to look on the net, where I would find out what the letters meant. So I did. They stand for Bachelor of Arts, an honour that is given to people who have contributed to knowledge and culture. This kind of title is what I have always wanted. I look on myself as a folklorist. Why should it just be people in academic circles who can do a dissertation on the Stewarts of Blair and get the honour of being called a folklorist, through our culture? Hamish Henderson always said, 'Sheila, you are a very important folklorist, and you should call yourself that', but I am afraid a lot of academics wouldn't agree with Hamish. All the same, I have worked as hard as they have to make travellers and their culture accepted in this world.

I would just like to say this about travelling people. We are not animals, as some people in society think we are. I have been a social worker and a liaison officer in Leeds, Sheffield and Bradford. I worked with the Secretary of State's committee on Scottish travelling people. I haven't much education, but, by God, I have knowledge and commonsense. And to get on in this world these are the most important things. I heard a quote from an Irishman lately that I liked very much. 'My goodness, that man is educated, but he has no brains.'

I quote Murdo Nicholson, the chairman of the advisory committee: 'Get to know these people as I do, and you will love them as I do.' He was one of the greatest men I have ever known, and so honest. There is more to travellers' ways than a dirty lay-by.

The first traveller man recorded by the School of Scottish Studies was Johnnie Faa. He came from the Borders, and according to our travellers' myth, he walked so far he walked straight to the gates of Heaven. This is to show that we are welcome in heaven, and God will let us in.

Then there was the traveller Macpherson, who was hanged in Banff. The executioners changed the time on the town clock so they could hang him before the pardon came through. His band of men stood there and watched their leader be hanged. Macpherson said to them, 'Who will stand up and be counted for me?' No one said a word, they just hung their heads. 'None of you will stand by me, so not one of you will get my fiddle.'

He broke his fiddle over his knee and threw the broken pieces at them. Then they hanged him for being a tinker man. In these days, if you said you were a tinker they would hang you.

Now, a few weeks later, the new leader of the band of travellers was William Tinkler. He gathered all the clan together round the fire, and said to them, 'The best leader we ever had was Macpherson, and we let him down. I feel so guilty about this I am willing to hand myself in, to honour his memory, and to stand up for him now and be hanged.' All the men agreed, and they gave themselves up. Each of the band, one at a time, declared they were tinkers, and they were all hanged.

The law that tinkers should be hanged was passed by a secret parliament in Edinburgh, long, long ago, and it never was abolished, even when the laws on burning witches and many others were abolished. Hanging for being a tinker wasn't abolished until they abolished hanging in Britain, and that's not that very long ago. But, to quote my mother, 'There will be travellers till the end of time, and you will never get rid of us.'

I hope you like my book. It is the truth. I am not dead yet, and there may be more to come. It was the hardest thing I have ever written, because I have had to go over the events of my life again, the good and the bad and the deaths in my family, which was the hardest thing of all. Maybe this book is not like other people's biographies. But it has to be different, and people will expect it to be different, because a traveller's life is different from anyone else's.

I will end with a poem. I was born into a world of poems and stories and songs, and I have heard them and performed them all my life. They have been my friends and my comfort. Because of them I have travelled round the world and been to see lands and people I never would have met otherwise, people who became my friends. Through keeping my tradition alive I have preserved the soul and culture of my people, the travellers' life that I love, although it has been a hard life at times. I will leave you with a poem that I wrote about one of these times.

It is about the day when travellers were evicted from the berryfields of Blairgowrie. When Hamish Henderson heard about them being put off the berryfield, he was so angry. He came to see us in Blairgowrie and said he wanted to take it further. We discussed it, and decided to fight the eviction in court, the high court in Perth.

Hamish had told the story to QC Lionel Daiches, who said he would take it on and he wouldn't take a fee. He said it was something he wanted to get his teeth into. The case was heard, and after Lionel had spoken for five minutes it was thrown out of court and we had won. The following year there were twice the number of travellers came to pick the berries. That was thanks to Hamish again.

I wrote this poem after the court case. I was only 16 then and it was about 1954. It is part of my travellers' legacy that I am leaving to you.

It's a Hard Life Being a Traveller

It happened at the berryfields,
When the travellers came to Blair,
They pitched their tents on the berryfields,
Without a worry or care.

But they hadn't been long settled there,
When some heed yins came fae Perth,
And told them they must go at once,
And get off the face of this earth.

These folk, of course, were worried,
For of law they had no sense,
They only came to the berryfields,
To earn a few honest pence.

But it was awfy hard to keep them there,
When the policemen said to go,

But they just packed up, and took the road,
To where I do not know.

It's a hard life being a traveller,
I have proved it to be true,
I have tried in every possible way,
To live with times that's new,

But we're always hit below the belt,
No matter what we do,
But when it comes to judgement day,
We'll be just the same as you.

Travellers' Cant

As you know, all my life I have carried a heritage on my back, and my life's work has been to spread it. It would not be right not to put my traveller's language in this autobiography. Not very many people use my kind of Perthshire cant now; the ones that used to are all dead. The kind of thing they used to say was, 'Pyre the been loor chates in the mort's clooishes' (Look at the nice earrings in the woman's ears). My kids know cant, but they don't speak it fluently to me, only a word here and there. This is a guide to the travellers' cant language, which they used in ballads, songs, and stories. I leave this as part of my legacy to all who are interested.

Alcoholic drink, *peeve*

Baby, *peekie*
Back, *doomy*
Bad, *shan*
Bag or sack, *blaswag*
Bagpipes, *stumers*
Basket, *scull*
Beef, *carnis*
Belly, *morikins*
Blood, *been yerum*
Boat, *beery*
Boil (kettle), *wammle*
Boy, *geddy*
Bread, *penum*
Breasts, *sucklers*
Brother or sister, *sprall*
Butter, *smout*

Car, *broskin*
Cart, *pursteegie*
Cigarette, *haa'in chate*
Clothes, *tuggery*
Coal, *yag*
Coat, *hinger* or *tug*

Corn, *grenam*
Corns (on feet), *grenum tramplers*
Cow, *rowtler*
Cup or bowl, *mazzy*

Doctor, *dodder*
Dog, *yaffin* or *buffert*
Door, *bellamint*

Eat, *haa*
Eggs, *yarrows*
Expensive, *shan loor*
Eyes, *winklers*

Face, *chackers*
Feet, *tramplers*
Fighting, *marin'*
Fire, *glimmer*
Fish, *flatern*
Food, *habbin*

Gamekeeper, *poosky coul*
Gentleman, *been coul*
Girl, *dilly*
Give, *feek*
Good, *beenship*

Hair, *fasum*
Halfpenny, *curdee*
Hands, *femmles*
Head, *test*
Hen, *ganney*
Horse, *grie*
House, *kane*
Hurt, *marred*

Kettle, *cookavie*
Knife, *choorie*

Larch tree, *lerrick*
Lice, *neet* or *parry*
Look, *pyre*

Mad, *moich*
Man, *coul, gadgie*
Man's private parts, *carry*
Married, *akumed*
Match, *blinkum*
Milk, *yerrum*
Minister, *been pattern*
Money, *loor*
Monkey, *swinger*
Non-travellers, *country hantle*
Nose, *neb*

Oh my goodness! *Ged dear*
Other one, *vavver chate*

Pee, *sloosh*
People, *hantle*
Pig, *gruffy*
Pocket, *porris*
Policeman, *ploop* or *feekie*
Porridge, *papplers*
Potatoes, *maglums*
Pregnant, *byuggent*
Priest, *been naskil*
Private parts, *juravil*
Put, *bing*

Rags, *feechils*
Rat, *longtail*
Ring, *grannie*
Road, *lig*

Shit, *geer*
Shoes, *strods*
Shop, *chova*
Silly, *mooch, thickent* or *cull*
Small child, *kinchin*
Small, *teekny*
Smell, *saver*
Snake, *wriggly*
Soup, *shach*
Spoon, *tullum*
Stew, *sloorich*
Sticks, *filshies*
Stone, *clach*
Stop or be quiet, *stall*
Sugar, *sweetnie*
Swearing, *salachin*

Take, *feek*
Tea, *weed*
Tobacco, *pluffin*
Toilet, *sloosh kane*
Traveller, *nakin*
Trousers, *brickets*
Turnip, *shnep*

Ugly, *rank* or *rump*
Unlucky, *insantifit*

Water, *monticlear*
Window, *withera*
Woman, *mort*
Woman's private parts, *blurt* or
   juravil
Wood, *baysh*